HILLSDALE

Greek Tragedy in
America's Heartland

Books by Roger Rapoport
Is the Library Burning? (with Laurence J. Kirshbaum)
The Great American Bomb Machine
The Superdoctors
The Big Player (with Kenneth S. Uston)
California Dreaming: The Political Odyssey of Pat and Jerry Brown
Into the Sunlight: Life After the Iron Curtain
I Should Have Stayed Home (co-editor with Marguerita Castanera)
After the Death of a Salesman: Business Trips to Hell

Travel Books
The California Catalogue (with Margot Lind)
2 to 22 Days in Asia (with Burl Willes)
22 Days Around the World (with Burl Willes)
Great Cities of Eastern Europe
Getaway Guide to Colorado
Getaway Guide to California

Children's Books
The Wolf
The Rattler

HILLSDALE

Greek Tragedy in America's Heartland

Roger Rapoport

RDR Books
Oakland, California

Hillsdale: Greek Tragedy in America's Heartland

RDR Books
4456 Piedmont
Oakland, CA 94611
Phone: (510) 595-0595
Fax: (510) 595-0598
E-mail: rdrbooks@lmi.net
Website: www.rdrbooks.com

ISBN 1-57143-088-1

Library of Congress Catalog Card Number 00-105739

Editor: Bob Drews
Text and Cover Design: Paula Morrison
Researcher: Ann Hagen
Cover Photo: Welcome Sign, Hillsdale, Michigan

Distributed in Canada by General Distribution Service,
325 Humber College Boulevard, Toronto, Ontario M9W 7C3

Distributed in England and Europe by Airlift Book Company,
8 The Arena, Mollison Avenue, Enfield, Middlesex, England
EN37NJ

Distributed in Australia and New Zealand by Astam Books pty Ltd.,
57-61 John Street Liechardt, New South Wales 2038

Printed in Canada

For Martha and William Ferriby

Lissa Jackson Roche

Table of Contents

DRAMATIS PERSONAE

George C. Roche III, President of Hillsdale College
June Bernard Roche, his First Wife
Dean Hagan Roche, his Second Wife
Margaret Roche (Granaw), his Mother
Margaret Ellen, his Sister

Children of George Roche III and June Bernard Roche
George Roche IV (called "Eye Vee")
Muriel Roche Peters
Margaret Roche
Jake Roche

George Roche IV's Wife
Lissa Jackson Roche

Child of George Roche IV and Lissa Jackson Roche
George Roche V

Lissa Roche's Family
Charlotte Jackson, Mother
Dr. Jack Jackson, Father
Laura Jackson, Twin Sister
Linda Jackson DelGobbo, Sister

Through the Hillsdale Looking Glass

O NE OF THE WAYS MY WIFE, Martha Ferriby, a library director living in Michigan, and I, a Californian, stay in close touch is through newspaper clippings. In this age of instant messaging, it's a nice change of pace to open a fat package filled with "local" stories about cockroaches destroying a wedding cake or a burglar suing for damages when he tumbles through a skylight.

In the fall of 1999, one of these packets included a *Washington Post* article by Jennifer Frey, reprinted in the *Muskegon Chronicle,* the paper where I began my career covering high school sports. As it turned out, I knew a little about the subject of the writer's fascinating story, Hillsdale College.

Founded in 1844 in Spring Arbor, Michigan, by Freewill Baptists from New England, the college began with five students and a single professor serving as president. During those pioneer years some students walked hundreds of miles to reach the new campus, where they studied by candlelight and slept on beds made from straw. Most made their living on farms. During the spring semester, enrollment dropped because many students had to return home to sow crops and tend livestock.

The college, originally called Michigan Central, was strongly anti-slavery and pro-temperance. Because the University of Michigan enjoyed a state-sanctioned monopoly over college degrees, students at private colleges could take instruction but not graduate. Not until the state legislature had a change of heart in 1850 did the school become Michigan's first private college to grant liberal arts degrees.

In 1853, after a spirited bidding war, the college trustees agreed to build a new campus at Hillsdale on a site nicknamed Piety Knob. Determined to hold onto their college, residents of Spring Arbor obtained a court injunction blocking the school's relocation. But a year later, the injunction was dropped and Hillsdale College rose at its new location. From the beginning, the college offered a curriculum rooted in the classics, with an emphasis on Plato, Socrates, Cicero, Homer and Tacitus. Students studied Latin and Greek, French and Hebrew, the sciences and mathematics. They were required to write and give speeches and pass exams administered by a visiting board.

To finance this new seat of higher learning, professors like Ransom Dunn left their positions in 1853 to raise the endowment necessary to keep Hillsdale College alive. His assignment was to bring home $10,000 from Illinois, Wisconsin, Iowa and Minnesota. Because there were hardly any railroads (even Chicago lacked rail service) and few decent roads or bridges, this evangelist journeyed mostly by horseback and stage to reach congregations that would become the cornerstone of his educational missionary work. Traveling with his family, the Dunns camped in tents before finally settling on a Wisconsin farmstead. From this base he spent two years out on the hustings scouring churches to build a subscription list composed largely of small donations in the $1 to $5 range. The largest gift was $100. Apparently few people objected to be being dunned by Dunn. And the astonishing $20,000 he raised inspired other Hillsdale field agents to solicit promising new territories to the south and east.

Ransom Dunn

This early success was crucial to putting Hillsdale on the map and making it Michigan's largest private college for much of the nineteenth century. Because the college opposed all discrimination, it attracted many Southern black students (Hillsdale had been a stop on the Underground Railroad) and opened its doors to students of all Christian denominations and Jews. Among them were students awarded scholarships in exchange for generous donations from their families. As a nonsectarian school chartered to educate students "irrespective of nationality, color or sex," Hillsdale aggressively promoted women to faculty and administrative positions.

As Hillsdale's reputation grew, so did its fiscal difficulties. The early struggles faced by Dunn and the college's founders persisted for a century. A low point came in January 1952 when the trustees were refused a $50,000 loan request by Hillsdale State Saving Bank, still smarting over interest lost when the college defaulted on some of its obligations in the 1930s. To remedy the situation the trustees promoted its chief fund raiser, J. Donald Phillips, to the college presidency in early 1952.

The former Michigan State University administrator struggled to cover the school's intractable deficit, leaning at times on a local druggist who dipped into his till to help the school cover payroll. A private man who liked to enter and leave his office via an exterior fire escape to avoid running into people he didn't want to see in the hallways, Phillips offered a startling vision.[1]

Phillips decided the best way to raise money was to actually turn down all state support. This contrarian approach began with the school's decision not to participate in President Eisenhower's National Defense Student Loan program. This shot across the bow began a grandiose campaign to sweep federalism off campus. The school's position hardened in the late '50s when Washington began beefing up college funding in response to Russia's Sputnik success in outer space. Eager to demonstrate its commitment to winning the space race, Congress appropriated several billion dollars for campuses coast to coast. From the research labs to scholarship programs, Hillsdale refused to accept government funding that appeared to compromise its educational mission. The trustees were not about to let this particular camel slip its nose under the campus tent.

In the history of American higher education, this was probably the most aggressive public stance, some might even call it libertarian approach, ever taken against government funding. Although free public education was a proud American tradition, Hillsdale had no trouble turning away from both Washington and Lansing in its quest for freedom. The trustees swore out a new Declaration of Independence looking to "students, alumni and friends who share their views" to "reaffirm (Hillsdale College's) historic independence and to resist subsidization of its affairs by the federal government."

"Every gift," cried President Phillips, "is a blow for freedom, hammering out a unified answer to those men who would have us sell our birthright."[2] Unfortunately this battle cry was not always answered. In 1964 total donations to the campus were just $13,000. Even though he was having trouble borrowing the funds necessary to cover faculty salaries, Phillips was "not tempted by the siren song of federal support and ultimate control that requires sacrifices on all our parts."[3] Taking the offensive, Phillips attacked President Lyndon Johnson's decision to boost federal aid for higher education to more than $3 billion. The fact that the bulk of this money was going to the physical sciences, at the expense of the humanities, was one more nail in the coffin of traditional liberal arts education. What good was a man on the moon if he couldn't quote Socrates?

To prove his point, Phillips crusaded to turn his campus into a role model for academe. While colleges across the country were at the heart of a protest movement that would challenge *in loco parentis*, fuel civil rights demonstrations and take on America's role in the Vietnam War, Hillsdale was so quiet you could hear a fraternity pin drop. The abolitionist hotbed of the nineteenth century was now the kind of place where a student could actually get kicked off campus for using a bullhorn at a campus rally. "It was almost as if the '60s didn't happen here," explained history professor John Willson.[4]

Almost, but not quite. "We did have one student meeting in front of Central Hall," recalled Willson's colleague Arlan Gilbert. "Three faculty spoke. Two spoke against the war and one spoke for the Vietnam War. This was in 1964 or 1965."[5]

Focusing on the future, Phillips was determined to make Hillsdale the centerpiece of a remarkable crusade against the dark decade of student protest. As National Rifle Association president and actor Charlton Heston would put it, "This isn't a college. This is a 1940 movie set of what a college ought to be."[6] Just add Mickey Rooney and stir.

The high point of Phillips' campaign came during the student revolution in 1968, the year that claimed Robert Kennedy and Martin Luther King Jr. In the 1950s football coach Muddy Waters and his team rejected an invitation to play in Florida's Tangerine Bowl because the host committee insisted that the team field only white athletes.[7] This kind of protest was the approach President Phillips had in mind when he issued his famous July 22, 1968, letter to students with the formality of a papal bull.

"Let it be known that any act of violence or intimidation, any seizing of any portion of property or any unauthorized activity which prevents the normal operation of the College in any way by any individual or groups of individuals will be considered in direct opposition to the necessary operation of the College, and action sufficient to the cause will be taken immediately ... (this letter) is submitted now in order that any student may still have adequate time to select another college if the above terms are not acceptable."

Phillips' reassertion of *in loco parentis,* coupled with the school's decision to reject federal funding because it threatened Hillsdale's independence, won the hearts and minds of donors to the delight of Hillsdale fundraisers. Many gifts came from donors who had never even seen the campus.

Phillips' letter, reprinted and excerpted in hundreds of newspapers and magazines, on television and radio, generated feature treatment in leading national publications such as *U.S. News & World Report.* He would be rewarded with a Freedom Foundation Award from the Nixon White House for his heroic effort. Less than a year later the school's board of trustees seconded his view.

"This is a private school. The purpose is to enroll superior students and to provide the finest education.... Disruption, obscenity and turmoil have no place in the process. Those who participate in or abet such activities are hereby given due notice that they are not welcome at Hillsdale College and activities such as those illustrated and of like kind, will not be tolerated and may be terminated by suspension, expulsion, termination and—as a last resort—force and criminal prosecution."[8]

While Students for a Democratic Society was launching its radical platform across the state with its Port Huron Statement, Hillsdale was busy countering the counterculture. The brave new world of Mario Savio, Tom Hayden and Jerry Rubin, the civil rights demonstrations in Birmingham and Montgomery and the riots at the 1968 Democratic Convention in Chicago were a world apart from Hillsdale, where the dean of men forced long-haired men to be shorn before allowing them to register for classes.[9]

Although political protest demonstrations did not occur at Hillsdale, the school was not completely out of the limelight. On the evening of March 21, 1966, more than 80 women living in McIntyre Residence spotted a flashing red and white UFO. This invasion, covered by the *New York Times* and *Time* magazine, was officially investigated by Northwestern University's famed astrophysicist, Dr. J. Allen Hynek. He dismissed the entire affair as marsh gas emanating from the school's treasured arboretum.[10]

Most of the reporters who descended on the campus for the UFO crisis ignored a bigger story. Hillsdale's politics were part of a backlash that presaged the end of Johnson's Great Society and Nixon's ascendance to the White House. Like Hillsdale, Nixon had campaigned hard against the leftist protest movement. His victory was an inspiration to the school's leader.

But fame—and fundraising—were fleeting for Phillips. Hillsdale's Operation Independence, created to raise $35 million for the college's 125th anniversary in 1969, delivered a disappointing $11 million. While Phillips succeeded in increasing faculty salaries, building the Dow Leadership Center and adding a new student center, science center, residence hall, preschool laboratory and many other facilities, the college was slipping back into the red. In May 1970, the trustees learned that Hillsdale was running its first deficit since 1957. Within a year the school had nearly exhausted its fiscal reserves.[11]

President Phillips suggested it was time to step down. The national search for his successor took more than a year as the trustees considered over 100 candidates. In 1971 they selected a 35-year-old historian named George Roche III, director of seminars for the Foundation for Economic Education in New York.

As president, Dr. Roche, during the next 28 years, raised over $300 million, recruited an outstanding faculty and made Hillsdale the darling of America's conservative movement. His daughter-in-law Lissa Jackson Roche managed national and campus speaking programs at the heart of the college's successful development program. Jeane J. Kirkpatrick, Margaret Thatcher, Thomas Sowell, Steve Forbes, Colin Powell, William E. Simon and Pat Schroeder were among the hundreds of celebrity guests she welcomed to campus. Through *Imprimis,* the campus speech digest she edited for 15 years, Lissa reached over 900,000 subscribers who were at the heart of Hillsdale's development campaigns.

These friends of the campus and thousands of students

who knew Lissa through the popular Center for Constructive Alternatives lecture series were stunned to learn of her death on October 17, 1999. Those who knew Lissa praised her as a thorough professional, a dedicated mother and aunt, a gifted editor, a generous and warmhearted individual who edited treasuries of Christian thought, a perfectionist dedicated to helping young people. Shortly after her funeral, President Roche resigned and was pensioned off, according to media reports, with a $2 million golden parachute. He left America's leading conservative college with no forwarding address.

Was there a dark side to Lissa Roche behind the accolades? I don't know. Like any of us, surely there was a side the public never saw. Indeed, about a month after her death, George IV, an adjunct history professor, physical therapist, expert woodworker and carpenter, firearms instructor and cyclist, gave an exclusive interview to the *National Review*. Known to everyone in town as "Eye Vee," he stated that hours before her death, his wife claimed to have conducted a 19-year affair with her father-in-law.

This was not the first sex scandal to hit Hillsdale College. In 1871 Henry Whipple, a professor of sacred theology, belles-lettres and rhetoric, was accused of violating the public trust. A college trustee who had raised significant sums of money for the school by working across Michigan, Indiana and Ohio, he helped build Hillsdale's first Freewill Baptist Church congregation. But his career at Hillsdale came to a swift end after a local woman stopped by to visit her friend Mrs. Bayless, glanced through a window and spotted the married woman cavorting with the good professor. Although rumors had circulated about Whipple's indiscretions for some time, this irrefutable evidence put an end to his denials. He resigned and moved to California after confessing his violation of the

Seventh Commandment. Years later Whipple apologized to the college for his mistakes and asked for forgiveness.[12]

But this time no *mea culpas* were being issued from Central Hall. The *National Review,* edited by William F. Buckley, a longtime friend of the Roche family and Hillsdale College, did not print a rebuttal from the president or the trustees. Daily newspapers and magazines across the United States picked up the story and reported on Lissa Roche's death. Eager to reclaim its reputation, Hillsdale College hired a new publicist and began running full-page open letters in the Detroit newspapers quoting that well-known first century B.C. pagan, Publius Syrius.

My wife had sent me a copy. "Prosperity makes friends, adversity tries them,"[13] said the advertisement. Recapping the good news at Hillsdale, the college pointed out that during her tenure, circulation of *Imprimis,* the speech digest Lissa edited, had jumped from a few thousand to 900,000. This boast struck me as a strange way to respond to the tragedy of her death.

"We were certainly unprepared for the intense media scrutiny that followed the retirement of our president and the loss of his daughter-in-law," the college explained to newspaper readers over their morning coffee. "People realize that events surrounding the former president and his family should not reflect on the quality of a Hillsdale education."

In the same ad the board of trustees caught my eye with their spirit of openness: "We look confidently to Hillsdale's future and invite you to share our sense of mission and purpose as we move forward."[14]

I slipped through the looking glass, courtesy of a Northwest Airbus. A few hours after leaving California on a red-eye, I woke up to a cheerful greeting from the flight deck.

"Welcome to Michigan," said the pilot. In just a few minutes Hillsdale would be showing up on the radar.

* * *

Hillsdale's Mitchell Public Library was closing down when I arrived late one winter evening, eager to orient myself to the southern Michigan town that had been Lissa Roche's home for nearly a quarter of a century. It was almost 8 P.M., far too late to start phoning for interviews. "If you wanted," one of the librarians told me, "you could go over to the bookstore. I think they're still open."

Located in a windowless brick building on the edge of downtown, Volume One was a bibliophile's dream—old *Life* magazines in cases, stacks of local history books, well-priced novels, paperbacks and even a few copies of *Winona,* the campus yearbook, well organized and well used. The owners, Richard Wunsch and Amy England, had been doing a brisk business selling the police report on Lissa's death. "A lot of people feel more comfortable buying it here than down at the police station," Richard explained while Amy reached for a fat scrapbook filled with hundreds of clippings, documents and e-mails gathered from the underground Hillsdale Liberation Front website as well as letters from former professors.

Glancing through the scrapbook I learned that Lissa Roche had edited more than 30 books, most of them for the college press. With a Central Hall desk just steps from her father-in-law's, Lissa had helped the president create a body of work that staked out Hillsdale's foreign and domestic policies on such core issues as federal funding of higher education, the federal deficit, free trade, academic freedom, feminism, free enterprise, race preference (a.k.a. affirmative action), student rights and responsibilities, *in loco parentis* and national defense.

Studying Hillsdale's endowment, which had soared from $1 million to over $300 million during the Roche era, it was clear that Lissa, on a first-name basis with statesmen and billionaires, famous publishers, Supreme Court justices and philosophers, was a development virtuoso. From the volunteer Hillsdale Associate Program to syndicated newspaper columns placed in papers by college loyalists across the land, Lissa Roche was also the Tom Paine of the Hillsdale revolution. When President Roche rose to wow a lecture audience, it was often Lissa Roche's carefully crafted language that echoed through halls from Los Angeles to Miami Beach. Her work was also critical to the success of Shavano Institute seminars, the college's Chautauqua-style gatherings held around the country. Audiences crowded in to hear the latest from speakers such as former Secretary of Education William Bennett and General Norman Schwarzkopf.

Lissa Roche was proud of the fact that Hillsdale was much more than a seat of higher learning. It was a place where students could step back in time and find out what the world was like before the advent of the birth control pill, the Black Panther Party and Title IX of the Civil Rights Act. Hillsdale College embraced the family values of Dan Quayle, the public policy of Ronald Reagan and the humanity of philosopher Russell Kirk. This was a campus where the yearbook featured photos of the school's John Birch Society chapter right next to the Lamplighters campus theater group.

Visiting reporters eager to write about Lissa Roche and Hillsdale had conducted some of their key interviews here at Volume One with helpful sources eager to protect their anonymity. Like a lot of people in Hillsdale, England and Wunsch were curious about the official story and the police department's decision to rule Lissa Roche's death a suicide.

Their questions were mirrored by many of the commentaries in their scrapbook. It appeared that it would take an entire day to copy their documents on the store's copy machine.

"Here," said Amy England reaching up for a thick stack of documents on a nearby shelf. "This is an extra copy of the entire scrapbook. Why not take it with you and save some time."

England's helpful attitude was mirrored all over town. Everywhere I went in Hillsdale, professors, friends of the family and officials opened their doors, eager to help. Among them was professor of Christianity and literature and former Dean of Faculty John Reist who invited me to Savarino's restaurant. He made a point of introducing me to friends at nearby tables, such as Chris Tsao, a popular professor of psychology who was doing a marvelous job of courting a potential donor from the south. Turning back to my host, I could see that he felt the matter of Lissa's death was not an open and shut case: "You know, I have a lot of respect for journalists. I used to be one myself in Chicago. You are the kind of people who can get to the bottom of things. That's what we need right now."[15]

As I listened to Dr. Reist, I considered the work of the Hillsdale police. With the help of laboratories and forensic officials from Lansing to Toledo, they had ruled that Lissa died of a self-inflicted gunshot wound to the right temple. IV's account of his father's alleged 19-year affair with his wife had already been thinly fictionalized in a "Law and Order" television episode.

Apparently the police, college administrators and some members of the Roche family all had an interest in closing the investigation of Lissa's death. But in their rush to judgment, the police had raised nearly as many questions as they answered. As I read the confusing and poorly written police report I imagined how Lissa, a consummate editor, would have reacted to all the typos ("brassiere" was misspelled) and Freudian slips (the police bought IV a "Whooper" at Burger King following Lissa's death), the twisted logic and half-baked detective work. The document concluded that she had died by her own hand. But when I finished reading the report, I felt that I knew less than when I had begun.

My search for answers to questions about Lissa's death began a few blocks away at Broadlawn, the opulent presidential mansion now shuttered as a trustees committee searched for George Roche's replacement.

1

A Couple of Kids from Colorado

"So come with George Roche to the shadow of Mt. Shavano, where the snow piles up over the rooftops and animals howl in the night and the road is closed for the season and even though your old friend drinks too much sometimes late at night, that is the time when he may have important truths to share, so you'd better listen. And then perhaps you'll know why Hillsdale is a better place than Harvard and why George Roche is a national treasure."
> —George Gilder in the introduction to
> George Roche's *A Reason for Living*

For Dr. Robert Anderson, the Hillsdale economics professor who credits himself with introducing George Roche to Hillsdale's board of trustees in 1971, history is not a judgment call. It is the truth written large by people who can see the past in a way that illuminates everything worth holding on to.

As a free-market economist with libertarian tendencies, Roche, director of seminars for the Foundation for Economic

Education (FEE), was a perfect fit for a school that blended a kind of John Wayne rugged individualism with the politics of Ronald Reagan. Operating independently of the federal government, Hillsdale was a safe harbor for professors like Anderson, who taught at Hillsdale for eight years. Like many of his colleagues, he can honestly say that his years at the small Michigan college were a highlight of his career. Shortly after arriving at Hillsdale in 1965, Anderson and his wife built a new home, and a few years later their two daughters were born. Along with his colleagues Dean Russell and John Sparks, Anderson taught an economics curriculum miles apart from the courses at Michigan State University and the University of Michigan in Ann Arbor. As free-market economists they were proud of a heritage that traced back to Adam Smith.

Because he had worked with Roche at the FEE, Anderson was delighted to recommend him to the Hillsdale trustees.[16] Anderson was convinced that his friend and fellow libertarian would bring several FEE colleagues with him to Hillsdale. He was also confident that Roche would find a way to actually complete the vision of his predecessor. While the school had raised money on the premise that it was a hotbed of conservatism, Anderson and other like-minded faculty members were not convinced. As he explained:

> The sad flaw at Hillsdale has been the massive public relations effort to create a conservative image which does not, and never has corresponded to the structure of its faculty. But we know that at Hillsdale the culprit has been far more than admission department rhetoric over the years. Of course, Hillsdale has had ... many fine conservative faculty

members. But the notion that the faculty as a whole has been conservative is absurd. We live in an age of extreme statism, and Hillsdale was not isolated from that reality. Statist politics dominate intellectual thought today, to such an extent that conservative ideas are rarely even heard in most college classrooms. The uniqueness of Hillsdale is that the conservative voice is being heard at all; but it was always a minority voice.[17]

One of the 35-year-old Roche's selling points with the board of trustees was his reputation as a powerful lecturer. Although he had only taught at the college level for two years, his FEE seminars featured name-brand conservatives from home and abroad. He was smart and funny and audiences were impressed by the breadth of his scholarship. His audiences didn't know that on occasion portions of his lectures were borrowed from FEE colleagues like economist Ben Rogge. For Dr. Rogge, it was a little like lending a cup of sugar to a neighbor about to bake a pie for a fundraiser. "I didn't mind him giving my lectures," Rogge told Anderson. "But he even stole my jokes."[18]

In the spring of 1971, after settling on Roche, the trustees asked to meet his wife. When June flew out to Michigan, she quickly realized this was merely a formality. "They were so impressed with George they would have hired him if I'd been a hippie, with a baby on my hip."[19]

Soon after he was hired by the Hillsdale trustees, Roche decided to purchase a silver Porsche 911 Targa. "I just can't object to this indulgence because he has worked so hard and this is something he has always wanted to do," June Roche told Anderson.[20] Barry Boyer, a conservative free-market economics professor who also came to Hillsdale from FEE, went with Roche, a certified car buff, to help him take delivery. He was delighted that George was picking out something nice until he discovered who was footing the bill.

"During the fiscal year 1971–72," recalls Anderson, "the administration had all of us on an austerity budget to keep the operating deficit to a minimum. Faculty were requested not to incur any expenses unless absolutely necessary. It was a 'belt-tightening' time at Hillsdale. So imagine my shock when it was discovered that the expensive sports car had been purchased at college expense, at George's request! The incredible indifference to the college's budget problem, not to mention his duplicity with me and others, confirmed for me his lack of integrity. We had learned what a master he was at conveying false impressions, and thus leading people to wrong conclusions. I never forgave him for that falsehood. It served also as an early example of his willingness to abuse his power."[21]

The first years of Roche's administration were beset with other problems. But in many ways these challenges were a kind of blueprint for Hillsdale's future. Inside each controversy was an opportunity for Roche, one that would open doors for many years to come. As the president explained, "We're probably the most politically incorrect school in America."[22]

George Roche III was born in Denver in 1935. His grandfather worked at the post office, rising to the level of superintendent. His grandmother, Dessa O. Hagge, was born in Fort Worth and, before moving to Denver, lived with her family in a sod house in Garden City, Kansas. In Colorado she worked for the Daniels and Fisher department store, moving up to a supervisory position in the china section. George Jr., the eldest of their two children, attended Westminster Law School and served in the Navy during World War I. In 1933 he married Margaret Stewart, the daughter of a Scottish mining engineer. She was born in the mountain town of Leadville, home of the famed Matchless Mine and the legendary Baby Doe Tabor, the impoverished widow of onetime mining magnate Horace Tabor.

George Roche Jr. made his living selling and setting up X-ray machines and physical therapy equipment at doctors' offices. A gifted salesman, he made a respectable living across the Colorado, Wyoming and Utah territory. Shortly before Christmas 1938, George Roche Jr. was delayed leaving an installation in Utah. Caught in a blizzard near Grand Junction, Colorado, he forged ahead in his Hudson despite the fact that most of the traffic pulled off the road and decided to wait until the storm passed.

Determined to make it home for Christmas, he headed up into the mountains, where a jackknifed truck forced him into a ditch. The car rolled over and landed upright. Even though the accident knocked out most of the car's windows, he decided to continue, wrapping himself in blankets, stopping in Salida for whiskey and coffee and continuing on the long slow ride home across South Park.

By the time he reached Denver, the salesman couldn't feel his hands or feet. While he made it home for Christmas, Roche Jr. paid a high price. Within a week he was being treated for pneumonia. In that pre-penicillin era, doctors treated him with sulpha drugs. The prognosis was poor and he spent the next six months in the "kickoff ward" at Fitzsimmons Hospital. "Your husband is a strong man," Roche's doctor told his wife. "Frankly he should already be dead."[23]

Not only did Roche Jr. recover, he was ready to go back to work in the spring of 1941. Unfortunately his old job was a casualty of the Pentagon. The federal government requisitioned his company's entire inventory for defense preparedness. To make ends meet, he took to the road for a series of stopgap jobs. The family moved to a rooming house near the railyard in Salt Lake City, where he did security work at night. From there they moved to Los Angeles, where he ran a creamery on Firestone Boulevard. Next was a job running a packing house in Torrington, Wyoming. Then the family moved to Greeley, Colorado, where Roche Jr. managed a Salvation Army store.

With their savings, the family put together enough money to buy a ranch in the Arkansas Valley near Salida. This 160-acre purchase, complete with horses and cows, was a bargain. Banks were eager to unload distressed properties. It was simply a matter of taking over payments, and of course, learning a new line of work.

The story of this purchase, thinly fictionalized in George Roche III's book *A Reason for Living*, suggests that his mother had her doubts about the move. The following account is from that book:

Pointing out that her husband knew nothing about ranching and was still plagued by health problems from his battle with pneumonia, she asked him:

"Why run the risk of a hard life on a ranch, especially after the doctor warned you that you couldn't work anymore?"

"But I *can* work, Fran! I've been getting stronger for the last year. I've been doing more and more in the store. I can do it!"

"You don't need to do it," Mom interrupted. "Why tempt fate? Why can't you ever be satisfied?"

"Because of the kids. They deserve a chance for something besides this damn store." Dad responded.

"You're such a dreamer—you're always looking for some magic land where everything will be perfect. Why don't you grow up?"

"I don't know what you call 'growing up.' But I do know our son and daughter are missing out on a lot of the experiences that mean *real* growing up," Dad bristled. "The way the world is going, those kids will needs roots more desperately than any generation before—far worse than you and I did. There's only one place to find those roots: the land...."

"Good Lord..., be a visionary, if you must, but don't punish your family!"

"Fran, when I was in the hospital and didn't expect to live, the main thought I had was that I'd let the kids down—that I wasn't leaving them with what they were going to need. I'm convinced that the best thing I can give the family, you included, is a sense of purpose, a sense of belonging. This ranch is the only chance I know to do that."[24]

For young George Roche III, the move was a grand adventure. "In those days, Salida was our primary shopping town. I well remember the drug store on the main street, complete with an old-time soda fountain. On the ranch we raised chickens for a little extra money and sold fryers to Jenny's Chicken-in-the-Basket, a great place to eat...."[25]

In 1944, George Roche Jr. and his father decided to make a play for the Princeton Hot Springs Resort. Leveraging everything they had, the two families offered the bank a pittance for the 440-acre property and hotel. "The deal must have happened on a day when the bank directors decided to cast off the mistakes of their predecessors," Roche III recalled years later. "We traded a broken down ranch by Adobe Park and a stone house in Denver for the resort. What we were trading was nothing compared to what we were getting."

Or so it seemed. The resort was a white elephant illuminated by coal and gas lamps. Rustic but not exactly charming, the ghostly hotel was quite possibly the largest fixer-upper in Colorado. The family moved to a lodge below the hotel on Chalk Creek Gulch. Here in the shadows of Mount Princeton and Mount Antero, the Roches began working on a plan to resuscitate the resort. They were fascinated by the hotel's history, particularly a woman named Mrs. Cole who had been operating the property for a bank.

"While she met with only moderate success as a hotel operator, she showed outstanding human relations ability," George Roche III would recall years later. "By her own public admission, she had married three times, once for the sake of art (Mr. Morton, a dancing teacher), once for a child (Mr. Benedict, a fine athlete, especially as a swimmer), and once for love (Mr. Cole, her current husband). While this may seem unusual, the real reality connected with this was that all three husbands lived simultaneously at the Antero Hotel during the time of Mrs. Cole's management. Most cordial relations prevailed as all worked on the property together and not infrequently enjoyed outings as a group. Mrs. Cole might have excelled as a marriage counselor," he wrote in a history of Mt. Princeton Hot Springs.

George Roche Jr.'s dream of creating a better life for his children in the mountains got off to a good start. Shortly after the family unpacked at their new home, his wife gave birth to a daughter, Margaret Ellen. While Roche Jr. and his father struggled in vain to put a dent in the hotel's deferred maintenance, George Roche III enrolled at the one-room Gas Creek schoolhouse. Attending class with 16 children spread across eight grades, he became part of a remarkable community.

In this valley sandwiched between a pair of peaks that created America's Continental Divide, families went to church, honored the Sabbath and most important "earned their way and spent their lives much as their parents and grandparents had in the 1800s," Roche III recalled years later. "The automobile, radio, the telephone and such had arrived, of course, but they really hadn't had much of an impact."[26]

This lifestyle was not limited to "some little backwater place that time forgot like Chalk Creek Gulch. This was the normal life shared by nearly all Americans. Across the country, in small towns and cities, even in the well-defined neighborhoods of the great metropolises, this was the way things were in the 1940s and into the 1950s. But there is more to it than that. It was in essence the life Americans had shared since the beginnings of the Republic and even before that, in the five generations of colonial life."[27]

Young George III had the run of the resort, living out a fantasy life in every room of the mountain hotel. He could cavort in the ballroom, act out on the stage, hang out on the vast front porch and run up and down the solid oak stairway. When he wanted to swim he could choose between one of four glorious pools. And when it was time to get serious he could hunker down in the beautiful library.

But behind this imaginary splendor lay a cruel fact: The Princeton Hot Springs resort was a wreck. "It was a shambles," recalls Dorothy Roman, an eighth-grade teacher who moved to Buena Vista in 1941. "In the 1890s it was a very elegant place. Three railroads ran 19 passenger trains a day, serving miners and tourists who came to enjoy the fabulous scenery and spa. People were entranced by the area. It was famous all over the world.

"By the time the Roches arrived, Chalk Creek Canyon was a dead area. You could buy places for back taxes. The old mining camps were ghost towns. The hot springs hotel was in terrible shape, it was a primitive spot without much furniture. It was like living in a deserted place."

In rural areas Chaffee County's young people were served by a network of 13 one-room schools. In 1941, at a community meeting considering consolidation, a local state representative eloquently summarized the case against building a new, larger district school. "I never went no further than the fourth grade and I done all right."[28]

At Gas Creek School, Roche III's teacher, Mrs. Georgie House, was a stern disciplinarian who didn't spare the rod to spoil the child. A conscientious instructor who had overcome much adversity in her personal life, she worked as a kind of stepmother to the children. Most emerged from eighth grade with an excellent foundation for high school.

Dorothy Roman, who lived in the area, saw the Roches as a class act, even if she didn't share their fundamentalism or conservatism. "George's mother was an intensely religious woman. . . . They believed in the healing powers of the love of Jesus. She and her husband were highly moral people who believed almost everything is a sin. They believed in the Ten Commandments, you don't steal, you don't lie, you don't commit adultery. It was all very biblical. They were an upright fundamentalist family that lived their beliefs. You couldn't imagine them doing anything wrong."[29]

While Roche III studied hard, his father and grandfather tried to sort through the fiscal wreckage of the hot springs. To make better use of the facilities, Roche Jr. invited his sister Dessamary and her husband Charles Black to open Mt. Princeton Commonweal, a private school for children from broken homes. Leftists who had studied at Columbia, the Blacks brought in students from Denver and other cities lashed by temptation and sin. These educators believed clean mountain air, the hot springs pool and, most important, a sound educational program would save these young people.

Understandably, there was nervousness around the Arkansas Valley about the possibility that some of these students would act out. Local residents were appalled when they learned that one of the students dumped a large jug of molasses into the hotel bar's piano. By 1950 the school was closed due to financial difficulties, and the hotel had gone dark. With squatters lighting campfires inside the building, the owners decided it was only a matter of time before someone burned the property down. In what amounted to a pre-fire sale, the Roches unloaded the landmark to an Abilene developer who carted off a million board feet of lumber to build a subdivision in that Texas city.

The hotel's demise was not quite the end of an era. For the next 10 years Roche Jr. continued to run Mt. Princeton Hot Springs as a summer resort. Guests were accommodated in the smaller hot springs lodge. Each fall the family returned to Denver where George III completed high school and enrolled at Regis College. In February 1955, the third-year college student married a Denver neighbor, 18-year-old June Bernard.

She was born in New York and lived there until the age of 10 when her parents separated. In 1947 she moved to Easton, Pennsylvania, with her father, who worked for a local newspaper. June knew many of the professors at Easton College and she enjoyed campus singalongs and sledding sponsored by school fraternities. Later she moved with her father to the Denver area where she met George.

In October 1955, June Roche gave birth to a son, George IV. The following year, after graduating from Regis College, Roche III joined the Marines. At boot camp a drill sergeant, dissatisfied with the way the Colorado recruit did pushups, stood on his back and derided Roche as a "college boy." The damage done to George's vertebrae would plague him for the rest of his life.[30]

In 1957, after returning to Colorado, Roche decided to enroll at the University of Denver law school. He abandoned that idea after one day, studied for a teaching credential and returned to Princeton Hot Springs with June and their son. For the next two years he commuted to Salida, where he taught American history in junior and senior high school. June helped make ends meet with a number of jobs including lifeguarding at the Hot Springs pool. The Roches sold the resort property in 1960 to another Texas developer named Dennis Osborn, who later married George's younger sister, Margaret Roche.

Roche loved teaching in the public schools. He also pursued a master's degree at night school, taking extension classes from state colleges in Greeley and Gunnison. Classmate Dorothy Roman, who also taught George's younger sister in Buena Vista, recalls Roche as an outspoken student. "His conservatism was very much in evidence. He spoke with great energy and enthusiasm. His moral standards when I knew him did not appear to be self-centered. They were centered toward the family, the community and the world in general."[31]

In 1958 he enrolled at the University of Colorado to pursue a doctorate in history. While he attended classes in Boulder, June Roche typed his dissertation on American policy at the end of World War II. She earned a degree in French literature at the University of Colorado in just over 2 years. Following graduation, June taught in the Jefferson County and Aurora Schools while George finished his graduate work in 1966. He was now Dr. Roche.

After George taught for two years at the Colorado School of Mines in Golden, he, June and IV moved to New York's Westchester County. June taught in the public schools at Dobbs Ferry while George ran the Foundation for Economic Education's seminar program. Traveling widely, the Roches were soon on a first-name basis with most of the economists who set up the Germany economy after World War II. From Milton Friedman to Friedrich Hayek, the seminars showcased the great conservative minds of the late twentieth century.

In his first book *Legacy of Freedom*, written while at the FEE, Roche suggested "something is deeply wrong with this world of ours" or as John Maynard Keynes put it, "Practical men who believe themselves to be quite exempt from any intellectual influences are usually the slaves of some defunct economist."

Inevitably this slave driver was, in Dr. Roche's mind, a sophist like Karl Marx, subverting morality and the rights of the individual in the name of collective society. As a humanist, Dr. Roche sided with Socrates. The sophists, really the first advertising men, were full of excuses because they could not understand the central premise of civilization, "that fixed standards of right and wrong existed independently of man."

This view got Socrates in trouble with the authorities. Nothing better symbolized his profound view of human nature, said Dr. Roche, than the way he handled his trial and death sentence. "Even at that moment, the serenity that comes to a man when he senses the truth and knows that he does came to Socrates." Responding to those who condemned him to death, the philosopher some people compare favorably with Christ, offered his own epitaph:

"'Be of good cheer and know of a certainty that no evil can happen to a good man either in life or after death . . . and now we go our ways, you to live and I to die. Which is better, God only knows.'"[32]

George Roche's enthusiasm for Socrates made him an ideal candidate for a college cast in the Greco-Roman tradition. After he was hired at Hillsdale, June decided to put her own teaching career on hold. One reason was that the couple's parental responsibilities doubled and soon tripled.

Shortly before moving to Hillsdale, George and June completed arrangements to adopt a three-year-old child in Seattle. Pausing at Hillsdale only long enough to drop off 15-year-old IV, they immediately flew to Washington to pick up their new daughter Muriel. Back in Michigan they settled in to a new home south of town on Baw Beese Lake. The Roches thoroughly enjoyed Hillsdale, its wonderful downtown office blocks and copper-domed courthouse, its beautiful churches, bountiful farms and hardworking citizenry. June found the town a great place to raise IV and Muriel, and a second daughter, Maggie, born the following year. She also enjoyed making a career shift from teaching to volunteer development work. Traveling to an endless series of Hillsdale events, June joked that there were two key aspects to fundraising, "Wear beige and smile a lot."

Moving in to the neo-Colonial campus mansion, Broadlawn, was a great leap forward for the family. "I was doing a lot of entertaining," said June. "Sometimes it was horrendous. In a single week we could do five lunches and five dinners." But the ceremonial aspects of running the big brick home on Hillsdale Street had many advantages. "I loved Broadlawn. I could buy flowers and develop a Japanese garden. Any time they tore down a building, I went over and saved the plants for our garden." The family built a lovely playhouse for the children and the front yard was distinguished by a giant Amer-

*George Roche III with June, George Charles Roche IV, 18,
Muriel Eileen, 3, and Margaret Clare, 1.*

ican flag flapping in the breeze. The Roches had finally reached
a point in life where money was not a big worry. "As long as
I could drive through the bank and get $200 and have a cou-
ple of credit cards, I was fine," June told her friends.[33]

From the beginning, the Roches hit it off with a who's who
of the conservative movement. Although he had never been
an academic administrator, those familiar with the new president had little doubt he could realize Donald Phillips' vision.
Among those on hand to celebrate his inauguration in October 1971 was *National Review* editor and *Firing Line* host
William F. Buckley. President Richard Nixon also sent his con-
gratulations: "Your new president and the College are obviously well suited to each other. It is gratifying to know that

this great institution will be guided in the years ahead by a man who has so aptly proved dedication to educational excellence and his sensitivity to academic values."[34] A future president, Ronald Reagan, who would one day appoint Roche to chair the National Council on Educational Research also sent the new president his best wishes. After 127 years of struggle it looked as if Hillsdale College was realizing the promise held out by its founders. Roche sounded a spiritual note as he lit out for what Huck Finn called "the territories."

A century earlier, Ransom Dunn had spent several years on horseback and foot, raising contributions for Hillsdale. Now George Roche was realizing Dunn's dream in a Porsche. Roche also took to the airways, visiting 23 states in the spring of 1972. In addition, he inaugurated impressive new seminar programs through the Center for Constructive Alternatives. Minds of the twentieth century such as George Bush, Margaret Thatcher, Czeslaw Milosz, and Malcolm Muggeridge would lecture on politics, history, journalism, sociology and education. Socrates, Benjamin Franklin and De Tocqueville would have fit right in at these free-for-alls that attracted both knee-jerk liberals and members of the vast right-wing conspiracy.

A modern educational missionary, often accompanied by his wife, Roche decided that the Hillsdale message was as critical as a 911 call. Those who could not send their children or enroll in one of the leadership seminars at the college's Dow Leadership Center could read the latest thinking of the school's leaders and distinguished guests for free in a speech digest called *Imprimis* (In the First Place). "It began with a thousand names George and I brought from the Foundation for Economic Education," recalled June Roche. "And as the list grew it created an enormous obligation. Just servicing the people who received it and wanted to meet with George turned out to be a big development job. He was addicted to his work and he had a strong sense of obligation."[35]

Despite problems with diabetes, Roche pushed himself, returning home from the West Coast on red-eye flights to host alumni at football games and, when necessary, cutting short vacations. At public events the trustees were delighted by the way Roche bantered with Hillsdale students. "I was fortunate to be young," the president told friends. "There wasn't that much of an age difference between me and the students."[36]

The fruits of his labors were easy to pinpoint. "He started with a college that had an almost nonexistent endowment and he turned it into a college with outstanding faculty that enjoyed high standards and good pay," says historian Arlan Gilbert. "When he came here there were no sabbaticals and no summer vacations for faculty. Now we have both. And in my 40 years on the Hillsdale faculty, including the Roche years, no one ever called me into the president's office and told me what to teach. It is true that George Roche knew what he wanted and he was not afraid to use his power and the kind of controls we have here to get what he wanted. I don't think any president can do that without having rebellion. I don't think we had gone toward a police state, far from it.[37]

"During Roche's second year on campus the faculty scheduled a vote on a unionization proposal. I recall his friend and number one advisor Louis Pitchford, telling me, 'If the union vote was positive, Roche and the trustees want us to shut the campus down.' That was George at his most determined."[38]

Roche's optimism was grounded in a clear understanding of the economics of academe. He could afford to be tough on the faculty because there were plenty of excellent candidates for new positions. He knew that Phillips' approach was a winner. For one thing it was unlikely that other schools could afford to lift Hillsdale's brilliant development concept. "They'd have to get rid of all the federal grants, which they can't do," explained economics professor Gary Wolfram.[39] As history professor John Willson told me: "You have to simplify to raise money. Our first successful campaign was the Freedom Fund, where the message was the simplest we ever used: 'Help us to raise the money we need to remain independent of federal control.'"[40] It worked.

Equally important was Roche's ability to sidestep the subject of how the money would be spent. "Roche didn't arrive here with a blueprint for a Stepford Village," added Willson. "The administration and the board of trustees decided to fight the government on filling out affirmative action forms. Our goal was to be independent, to do whatever we wanted. We could have started a '60s hippie commune if we'd wanted to."[41]

Like her husband, June Roche was intuitive at development work. "Really we were just a couple of kids from Colorado. . . . We produced a good product and we were able to secure money and developed our own style of doing it. We thought of ourselves as the Hillsdale family, we had donors and developed a school they were quite happy with. We had a really good faculty and academic program. Sure, kids party and once in awhile a girl gets pregnant, but that doesn't mean we weren't successful. We offered an alternative . . . we didn't just waltz down the path everyone else did."[42]

Friends like Robert Anderson were shocked to discover that Roche was also a tough administrator. "His winning charm and warm manner were traits, or should I say skills, such as I've never known in any other person. He was an incredibly engaging individual, the kind of person in whom you willingly put your trust, and he knew it and he used it. I've often reflected that, if there is a Satan doing his evil handiwork through us, George is just the kind of guy he would recruit.

"One of the first indications that there was a different man behind the facade was George's intolerance toward criticism. Some people can handle negative comments better than others, but George could not accept any. Like most narcissists, George had an insatiable appetite for praise but a zero tolerance for the slightest disapproval or even a differing judgment. Undoubtedly this flaw had much to do with his wrongful treatment of his wife, June, over the years. June is a gracious lady of the 'old school' who suffered silently through horrendous and repeated verbal abuse at the top of George's lungs. All of us knew of his hidden and extraordinary temper, in stark contrast to his public image. You learned quickly the futility of 'arguing with George' or even disagreeing with him. One hundred percent approval and agreement were required."[43]

Anderson experienced Roche's temper firsthand when he confronted the president in early 1973. Returning from Christmas vacation he learned that Clarence Carson, the History Department chair hired in spring 1972, had been terminated because the president wasn't comfortable with his work. At Roche's office, Anderson learned that the subject of Carson was not open to discussion. When he ignored Roche's warning, the professor was told, "If you don't like it here, you should leave too."

"I have tenure and don't have to leave, so why don't you leave?" shot back Anderson. By the end of the year Anderson had resigned and taken a job at the Foundation for Economic Education.

After Anderson returned to the FEE in New York, the foundation received a letter "from one of our contributors reprimanding us for sharing our donor list with Hillsdale. He was certain we were guilty, since the same mailing address error appeared on both of his envelopes. It confirmed something we had long suspected. As a member of FEE's board, George received our confidential monthly donor report. From the beginning at FEE we had supplied this information to trustees so they could know who was supporting our work, and, if they wished to do so, could contact the donor with a further expression of gratitude.

"Upon discovering that George was using our confidential donor list for fundraising activities at Hillsdale, we were forced to change our policy of sharing this information with the trustees. Thereafter, we supplied only a 'summary' of monthly donor information, deleting the addresses of our contributors. George's improper use of our confidential donor list violated his stewardship duty as a FEE trustee. It was another instance of his brazen disregard of ethical standards."[44]

Dr. Roche was so well connected in the conservative community that it is likely *Imprimis* would have flourished without the FEE names. And even if the accusations were true, the fact remained that the donors were giving their money to Hillsdale voluntarily. They liked what they were getting. Supporting Hillsdale's new Mossey Library, for example, made more sense than donating money to the athletic department at Michigan State.

Anderson was also critical of Roche's claim that the school had never accepted any federal funding. Many professors, such as Barry Boyer, the economist who helped the president pick out his Porsche, challenged Roche on this matter. Boyer's criticism was muted by the fact that his contract was not renewed in 1973. But his view was seconded by others including the Department of Health, Education and Welfare in Washington. In 1972 Congress passed Title IX of the Civil

Rights Act, banning discrimination in any federally funded education program. At first this law did not appear to apply to Hillsdale because the school did not accept any direct federal funding. But in 1975, new regulations stated that any college with students receiving federal money was a "recipient institution" subject to Title IX. Hillsdale's problem was that roughly 200 students individually received about $300,000 in government aid.[45]

The Hillsdale board of trustees handled this problem by passing an October 1975 resolution refusing to comply with Title IX. "We were graduating women and blacks more than a century before the federal government decided to get into the equal opportunity business," declared George Roche. "Women have been serving on the Hillsdale board of trustees, continuously since 1893. Hillsdale was the first college in Michigan, and one of the first in the nation, to elect a female trustee and to employ women as faculty members.

"The college had a showdown with federal officiousness as early as World War I. An army lieutenant ruled that a black student, though otherwise qualified, could not serve in the regular Hillsdale R.O.T.C., but would have to be inducted into a Negro unit. This touched off a flurry of telegrams between (Hillsdale) President Mauch and a War Department committee, resulting in final instructions to (the lieutenant) to follow the age-old Hillsdale practice of treating individuals without regard to color or creed."[46]

A tribute to Phillips' vision, this showdown became the cornerstone of a Hillsdale crusade that brought in support from across the land. Making its position known by sending out 40,000 letters to college allies and the media, the school declared that "Hillsdale College will, to the extent of its meager resources and with the help of God, resist by all legal means this and all other encroachments on its freedom and independence."

Or as Roche liked to tell audiences from sea to shining sea, "The day private colleges began accepting funding from the federal government, they ceased to become private." Privately, Roche elaborated in his best John Wayne manner: "When I ran into higher education, I saw a lot of ideas I did not respect. I had grown up in a conservative cul-de-sac. Anyone who came on your place, not as a friend but as someone who wanted to disagree, they better walk."[47]

National media coverage in *Time* magazine, the *New York Times*, and the *Wall Street Journal*, as well as attention from the electronic media, triggered support from across the land. Some donors contributed a portion of their Social Security pension. "Give 'em hell, George!" wrote another backer who enclosed a generous check. Equally impressed was economist Milton Friedman who declared, "Hillsdale is fighting for the freedom of all of us."

In March 1976 the Department of HEW's civil rights office wrote back that Hillsdale's participation in government-funded work study, grant and student loan programs meant that the school was governed by Title IX. Eager to find a way out, the trustees decided that they would have to start preparing for the day when Hillsdale students could no longer accept federal financial aid. A three-year fundraising campaign designed to raise $29 million began in the fall of 1976 with celebrities like Joseph Coors, Clare Booth Luce, William F. Buckley and William E. Simon on hand.

Adding a sense of urgency to the fund drive, HEW announced in December 1977 that it would begin enforcement proceedings against the school for its failure to comply with the legal requirements of Title IX. Those were fighting words for Roche, who told Jane Pauley in a December 1977 "Today" show interview that Hillsdale had no intention of complying with the government order. "We don't discriminate against women at Hillsdale. The first woman in Michigan and the second in the U.S. to receive a bachelor's degree received it at Hillsdale in 1851."

The school's historic stand was mirrored by an extraordinary scene at Central Hall. For the first time in campus history, and possibly the last, students formed a real picket line complete with placards. The college that had gone all the way through the Vietnam War without a single protest rally was now taking to the streets. "Standards Not Standardization," said one placard. "In George We Trust," insisted another.[48]

Although Hillsdale ultimately lost its battle in the courts, Roche was not deterred. "HEW did us a favor," he recalled years later. "It was easy to stand up and cry halt. We were glad to carry this idea along."[49]

Thanks to the support of sympathetic donors and alumni, Hillsdale raised enough money to replace federal aid with privately funded scholarships. Part of the makeup amount also came from student loans secured by the school's burgeoning endowment, another example of the campus's creative financing.[50]

Roche's resistance to Title IX reflected, in part, his distrust of government efforts to regulate the private sector. His opposition to comparable worth laws was based on his conviction that they are "anti-female. Insofar as bureaucrats set their pay over market rates, women lose jobs and opportunity." Federally funded day centers were an "assault on marriage and the home, and a brutally expensive one. Lost in all this frenzy of do-goodery is what it means for a woman to try to be a man— a thing by nature she cannot do."

Citing the pioneering work of George Gilder in his book *Sexual Suicide,* Roche pointed out that "society depends on having two sexes ... which is not to say that one sex or the other is superior ... just different. Most of us hugely enjoy the difference!

"Among the implications is that a male has a biological interest in taking the childbearing powers of more than one woman. He would, if permitted by law and custom, keep a harem.... In our own life we see this happen when a man divorces his wife and marries his young secretary."

Roche was also outspoken against the "ideological forces of our time" that "conspire against the conventional woman's role and marriage. Cohabitation is routine. Casual sex is approved. Divorce has been liberalized, in both law and custom, to the point of destroying our concept of permanent marriage. Alimony laws have been repealed. Oh yes, you've come a long way, baby. But are you better and happier than you were?

"It is the male who is liberated and the female who pays most of the price. Sexual liberation is expensive. As the coarse old saying had it, why pay if you can get it free? If she expects a commitment or even gratitude, she will be disappointed. She has by her own choice liberated the male from marital obligations; in reality from being a man."

And who exactly benefits from this sad state of affairs? "The political left thinks it does," said Roche. "It knows that normal relations between man and woman, and the families they create, both moral in nature, are fierce bulwarks against the dreamy utopian schemes it would like to impose upon us. Therefore it seeks to destroy both and it does so with a silky, siren call to be really free, beyond any natural or moral limits.... It is a scam. It is a scheme to destroy what means most to us, and to make us dependent upon the state.... It feasts on our every departure from moral behavior. Wouldn't it be easier (not to mention cheaper) for us to love one another, and to behave?"[51]

2

"I Married the Wrong George"

"If college catalogs were subject to false advertising laws, all college administrators would be in jail."
—Robert Anderson

I<small>T'S EASY TO BE SEDUCED BY</small> H<small>ILLSDALE</small>, where the 7-Eleven closes on some nights at 6 P.M. You have to laugh when Girl Scout leaders go on local radio stations to invite everyone to stop by their booth at a local "Taste of Hillsdale" food fair to "give us a bite."

In a state where many city slickers don't even realize Michiganians live south of Interstate 94, Hillsdale is proof positive that the still waters along the Indiana/Ohio border run very deep. This 50-mile-wide region south of towns like Ann Arbor, Jackson, Battle Creek and Kalamazoo includes some of the state's most beautiful scenery, including the lovely Irish Hills. Little Hillsdale is prosperous, picturesque and has a wonderful sense of humor about itself and the world at large. And like people in many college towns, Hillsdale's residents are perfect hosts. Newcomers can count on a warm reception. From the Hunt Club to Savarino's, Hillsdale is the kind of place where townspeople take guests to lunch or dinner and wouldn't dream of letting them pick up the check. Try it on your first visit and you're likely to get your hand slapped.

Although Hillsdale was founded by Freewill Baptists, agnostics and atheists can feel comfortable here, particularly if they are libertarians or Randian objectivists. Many conservatives are in the student body, but there's also plenty of room for those who are decidedly apolitical. Democrats have even been sighted on campus.

Hillsdale's branding, its effort to align itself with Republican causes, the Austrian school of economics and crusades like ending "race preference" (affirmative action) in college admissions certainly have benefited the entire enterprise. Could there be another college recruiting brochure in the land featuring both Vice President Dan Quayle (his father served as a trustee), and William F. Buckley? The impressive Hillsdale catalog is filled with quotes from giants of government such as former U.S. Attorney General Edwin Meese III, who considers "Hillsdale to be a beacon of enduring values that stands out amidst the foggy mists that sometimes enshroud higher education in this country."[52]

While the campus is overwhelmingly white and totally opposed to race preference in the admissions department, there is plenty of diversity when it comes to issues like religion or economics. It would be a mistake to assume that every student who enrolls at Hillsdale is focused on the philosophy of campus idols like Russell Kirk or the wit and wisdom of Whittaker Chambers. Each applicant comes with his or her own special reasons for choosing Hillsdale, including come-ons that the marketing department doesn't even consider when it lays out the school's recruiting brochures.

For Lissa Jackson it wasn't the photos of blooming dogwood at the arboretum or shots of a barefoot young woman propped up against an oak quietly reading Jane Austen that prompted her to apply in 1975. It was a picture of a handsome man in his 40s and his good-looking son. "I'm going to marry that man," she said confidently.

Realizing her ambition was a little like joining the Peace Corps, the cause looked like a good one, but there would be a few sacrifices along the way. Lissa, who grew up in California and finished high school in Florida, would have to head inland to the Rust Belt, giving up metropolitan life for a small-town existence. Unlike her twin sister Laura, Lissa Jackson was passionate about politics. Laura, who would become a successful artist, was more ethereal, the kind of Californian who probably would not have transplanted well to Middle America even if she listened to "Prairie Home Companion" every Saturday night.

Like George Roche's Porsche, Lissa Jackson generated interest from the day she arrived on campus. People were always asking questions about her. And, of course, she was asking a lot of questions herself. Like many newcomers, she didn't realize at first that Hillsdale was the kind of place where people often came for a short visit and ending up remaining for a lifetime. In the 1840s, a stalled railroad construction project meant that Hillsdale was literally the end of the line. While travelers were no longer getting stuck here, many longtime residents declared it was still a hard place to leave. Even professors who got in fights with the administration and moved away for better jobs did so with mixed feelings. Leaving often proved harder than it looked. And many of those who did leave often wished they hadn't.

Like many of the politically incorrect young people who came to Hillsdale, Lissa was brilliant and bound for glory. She was also a beautiful, slim, gray-eyed blond. During her high school senior year, the Californian had gone away to the Flint School in Florida, where students studied aboard a sailing vessel in the Caribbean. Referred to as "White Squall High," this floating boarding school attracted an eclectic group. Lissa liked to joke that she was the only student in Flint's history to enroll voluntarily.[53]

The fact that a lot of the students read Ayn Rand closely prompted some of her friends at Hillsdale to believe she was an objectivist. In fact she was politically eclectic, fascinated by a wide range of philosophers, poets and Christian theologians. A quick study, and a good listener, Lissa showed compassion and an extraordinary willingness to take on the problems of others. She was destined to play a role that would ultimately blend the humanity of Mother Teresa with the sex appeal of Katharine Hepburn.

"Lissa had problems with her father, a doctor who was very domineering," said campus historian Arlan Gilbert. "At the Flint school students were taught to have more inner strength." Clearly she applied this lesson at Hillsdale where she completed a degree in English with a minor in art in just two and a half years. Although Lissa had been dating her classmate IV since the fall of 1975, President Roche persuaded them not to rush into marriage. They waited until two days after graduation in December 1977. Dr. Roche paid for the wedding.

Close family friends such as Arlan Gilbert who lived with his family directly behind Broadlawn wondered if IV could keep up with his brilliant wife. "I don't think IV came anything close to Lissa's intelligence," he said. "Unlike Lissa, who took a B.S. degree, IV took a B.L.S. degree that exempted him from the school's foreign language requirement. George III was glib on a lot of subjects. IV was glib too, but there was no content."[54] Looking back on her decision years later, Lissa turned the subject into a great joke at her husband's expense. "I married the wrong George," she told friends with a laugh.

The newlyweds moved to California's Lake Tahoe for a year. After returning to the Midwest, IV taught English at Culver Academy for several years while Lissa took her master's degree at Notre Dame. Although IV did not have an advanced degree, he was hired as an adjunct professor in the Hillsdale College History Department teaching two sections of American heritage with a focus on ideology, constitutional principles and economics. Sports-minded, he decided to begin taking courses in exercise physiology at Michigan State. In 1986, he moved into a new office in the George Roche Education and Sports Complex, helping patients recovering from knee surgery and heart problems, developing exercise programs and performing fat tests. IV loved his work and his patients adored him. When the college decided to add a semester of western heritage to the American heritage course, adjunct instructor IV was happy to teach the new curriculum.

When historian Gilbert asked Lissa how her husband felt about teaching the broader course, she said, "Man, would he love to have your notes."

But after teaching the class for three semesters IV was nonchalant about the challenge. "You know how the freshman are," he told Gilbert. "They don't know anything. Teaching this course was a snap."[55]

While IV did physical therapy and taught, Lissa joined Central Hall's inner sanctum. As managing editor of *Imprimis* and the school's publishing division, she became a key figure on Hillsdale's development side. Students knew her best through her work at the Center for Constructive Alternatives. Eight to 10 events annually featured prominent speakers on a variety of timely issues. Lissa graded a deluge of student papers themed to these events.

The president and Lissa, both workaholics, continued to put in long hours at the office, vacation together with their families in Michigan and the Rockies and travel together to the Shavanos in Colorado, a scenic setting that grew into dreams of an intellectual magnet. Like many of Roche's contributions to the Hillsdale campus family, the Shavano Institute was inspired by a visionary. His name was John Andrews, a young man out of Buena Vista, Colorado, who had fallen in love with Roche's columns published in the local *Chaffee County Republican,* a paper run by an outspoken country editor named Gibby Gregg.

"George is nine years older than I am," said Andrews. "When I was living in Buena Vista, George was a college professor." It was a case of "hometown boy makes good. Not too many Ph.Ds come out of the one-room school at Gas Creek. There is young George writing these essays about current events. His first book, *Legacy of Freedom,* is a terrific survey of how our institutions and our ideas came down to us. George Roche was a famous name to me and it was a mouthful with a Roman numeral on the back."

Despite his success at Hillsdale, Roche had begun feeling restless and considering career alternatives. In 1978 the Hillsdale president dipped a toe in the political waters with a Roche for U.S. Senate committee.

"Ultimately the libertarian in George Roche formed by Leonard Reed and the Foundation for Economic Education in New York is uncomfortable with active engagement in politics," Andrews recalled. "He began to see that the kind of image makeovers and submission to political handlers and compromises of your beliefs that are required to compete for elective office was bad for the soul."[56] Citing his back problem, Roche dropped out of the running.

Three years later Andrews came to Roche with an idea that would bring Hillsdale's conservative idealism to a national audience. One day the Coloradan was "reading *Imprimis* and loving it. I couldn't believe how good it was and I couldn't believe a liberal arts college was doing this in terms of ... other colleges ... selling out the core idea of what America was." Andrews wrote Roche, mentioning his Buena Vista past, that he had been a speech writer for Richard Nixon and that his uncle was a congressman. In this letter he added that his alma mater, Principia College, hadn't stayed true the way Hillsdale had.

In February 1981, Andrews met with Roche and suggested that the college launch a new Colorado-based institute named for Mt. Shavano. Roche rejected the idea initially. But after thinking it over, he decided that moving back to Colorado and forming a conservative counterpart to the famed Aspen Institute made perfect sense. He would leave Michigan and go home to Colorado to run the program.

"He was thinking he had kind of plateaued," said Andrews, "that he had gone as far as he was going to go." But there was one important obstacle with the idea of quitting Hillsdale to head back west and initiate a seminar program with Andrews. The college trustees refused to accept his resignation. Hillsdale's president went back to Andrews with a counterproposal. He suggested setting up the new outreach program as a division of Hillsdale College in Colorado. At an initial organizing meeting in Vail during the summer of 1981, the project was given the green light and the Shavano Institute opened a Denver office in the fall. Andrews, who took charge, said, "The thought was he would come when we needed him to assist us with development efforts, at which he is a master."[57] Roche, of course, hoped that one day he might be able to find a way to shift his base to Colorado.

When Hillsdale College vice president Ron Trowbridge left the school to take a job in Washington with the U.S. Information Agency, Andrews was recruited to come to Hillsdale. He became the vice president for outreach programs, editing *Imprimis*, running the Center for Constructive Alternatives and spending the balance of his time back in Colorado running the Shavano Institute.

When the new institute found it difficult to persuade participants to travel to Colorado, Roche scrapped a plan to move the institute to a mountain lodge headquarters. Hillsdale began taking the Shavano seminars to cities and resorts around the country. This fruitful approach not only lured new donors, it was also an excellent platform for the school to showcase its brain trust to parents of prospective students.

Roche would sum up his eagerness to return to Colorado in a novel called *Going Home*. This book, "a memoir in form and fiction in method," is written as a confessional by a disillusioned New York businessman named George. In the book's foreword, Andrew Lytle writes, "We have the hero lost in the world of materialism, rejecting this to return to a cabin in the Rockies where he hopes to recover what he has lost."[58] George's best friend in the book is Gibby Gregg, a buddy who relives the good old days with the book's hero over a tumbler of bourbon in front of a roaring fire. There was a real Gibby Gregg in Buena Vista, the newspaper editor who published Roche's newspaper columns after he became an educational statesman. According to Ed Quillen, a Salida editor and *Denver Post* columnist who published the real Gibby Gregg's writing at the end of the newspaperman's career, this journalist did not take kindly to the red pencil. "When Gregg described the lieutenant governor of Colorado as a 'nigger,' I cleaned it up. He claimed I censored him, took the story back and quit writing for me."[59]

Roche's dream of moving back to Colorado was killed outright when the board relocated the Shavano office. "Ultimately," said Andrews, "the decision was that there was no need for a Colorado office. He (Roche) would run it from Michigan and it wouldn't be a physical entity. It would be a banner to identify off-campus speaking programs."

The Colorado staff and base of financial support that had coalesced around the Shavano Institute waned. After turning down a chance to move back to Michigan, the employees opened the Independence Institute, an independent free market think tank that issues recommendations for state and local government in Colorado.

Andrews ran the Independence Institute from 1985 to 1993, with time out for an unsuccessful run for Colorado governor on the Republican ticket in 1990. "I had nothing to do with Hillsdale in those years," he recalls. "Roche inspires intense loyalty and he expects intense loyalty from the inner circle. The corollary is that those who leave are in the out group. I liked the man so much and thought so much of the institution that in the course of time we solidified our friendship. For a period of time when I was absorbed in what I was doing here, there was a sense of disappointment in terms of what happened.... The essence of me is that I won't compromise. The more political I became, the more our views just diverged.... We needed to go off and cool our own tracks."[60] In 1998 Andrews won a seat in the Colorado state senate.

To Andrews, Roche was an extraordinarily gifted communicator and organizer, an "intellectual entrepreneur. Someone like that tries out different ideas and roles, and some of the rough drafts have validity."

No one knew more about George's rough drafts than Lissa. After Anderson and his staff departed, the president tapped her to run the Shavano Institute for National Leadership. Under the direction of Trowbridge, who had returned from Washington, she also served as managing editor of *Imprimis* and the Hillsdale College Press,which published reprints of Roche's books and a number of new titles about education, bloated government, history and economics. Anyone of significance who came to speak at Hillsdale knew Lissa Roche, the woman who made all the arrangements and frequently edited their remarks for publication in *Imprimis*. She also helped her father-in-law with a column that appeared in newspapers with a combined circulation of more than 2 million, thanks to the hard work of Hillsdale Associates. These loyal volunteers persuaded hometown editors across America to carry Roche's work.

Thoroughly professional and protective of President Roche, Lissa also guarded her own privacy on and off campus. She kept her distance from those eager to know more about the president, June, IV and herself. A number of faculty members felt she was too close to her father-in-law. When she fawned over Roche, some were nervous. Others suggested that their hugs went on a beat too long. More than one considered suggesting that he try to keep his distance from Lissa in the manner of a college professor quelling the ardor of a young student. But each, in their own way, decided not to share their concern.

Back home in Colorado old friends began wondering about Christmas cards featuring the family on the Broadlawn staircase. George and Lissa were photographed together on the front step while June and IV were parked in the back with the grandchildren. At times Lissa and IV felt crowded by the fact that their apartment over the student health center was located next door to Broadlawn. She was particularly dismayed by the president's tendency to walk over each day for a visit.

Lissa's friends agreed that the hard-working editor and seminar director was overworked and underpaid. Understandably, she complained about her family's finances. "She should have been paid $50,000 to $60,000 (a professorial salary)," said Gilbert.

"Salaries are a very carefully guarded secret here and Lissa was a very private person who never revealed her deep feelings. But one day she said to me, 'This job, I'm not getting paid what I deserve.' She had this thing about money. A number of times when money came up, she made it a real issue. Let me give you an example. When my third book for Hillsdale College Press was nearing completion Lissa wanted to know the completion date. She explained that it had to be included in her budget for that year. I thought that was strange. I just figured that whenever I finished the book they would move some figures around and publish it. But she said no, the money would have to be raised from a donor through John Cervini, the vice-president for institutional advancement. When I finished, I went to her and said I would like to donate $10,000 toward the publication of this book that would cost a total of about $25,000. She just jumped for joy."

Gilbert believes that Lissa's financial situation was complicated by the fact that her husband probably never earned more than $15,000 a year from his teaching and physical therapy work at the college. "President Roche wanted them to remain next door to Broadlawn. Lissa told me: 'IV and I have to get away from George, but I know he is not going to take it very well.'

"About two months later they moved to the college-owned stone cottage at 291 Hillsdale Street. When I went to see her there was nothing said about freedom from her father-in-law. This little stone cottage was not adequate for IV, Lissa and their son George V. She made a couple of comments about not being able to afford to buy a house like other couples. They were frustrated."[61]

Lissa's own writing and collections demonstrated a sense of humor. As the editor of books on the Austrian school of economics, she was an impressive factotum. On the phone with celebrity authors she could be demanding about deadlines and editorial changes. Her sarcasm prompted some to think her insensitive or cruel. But for those who knew her best, friends and family alike, Lissa was also full of kindness, a woman who went way out of her way fighting battles that appeared unwinnable. At times she would play mixed roles such as a mentor to a much younger brother- in-law, nurse to IV's grandmother ("Granaw") and best friend to her father-in-law.

What's important is the way Lissa Roche's death took a secure institution, firmly set in the bedrock of higher education, and turned it inside out. While the college was focused on the ever-present danger of civil rights legislation and federal scholarship regulations, it was a family matter that would test Hillsdale's legendary independence. Ransom Dunn, Donald Phillips, even George Roche himself could never have imagined that one woman's unchecked loyalty would turn the campus into a Greek tragedy worthy of Euripides.

3

The Ring of Gyges

*"It is appalling to think how fast the family in the
Christian sense has disappeared."*
—Andrew Lytle's introduction
to George Roche III's novel *Going Home*

"I NEVER ASKED PEOPLE FOR MONEY," said Roche, who raised
so much that even he couldn't be sure of the total.
Although they didn't always see eye to eye on the issues of
the day, every donor, each in his or her own way, contributed
to the miracle at Hillsdale.

Libertarians were attracted by Hillsdale's heterodoxy.
Free-market economists liked the idea that they wouldn't per-
ish if they failed to publish. Scientists were delighted to know
that they wouldn't be penalized for teaching instead of bringing in fat research contracts. Students knew that Hillsdale
operated, in Roche's phrase, "entirely outside the circle of
political correctness."

All this made parents feel reassured when they pulled up
to the campus teeming with eagle statuary compliments of a
key donor. One of the advantages of a Hillsdale education

was the fact that students weren't bombarded with radical chic reading lists or assaults on the "racism" of Mark Twain. The problem with this approach, as historians like Keith Windschuttle had pointed out, was that it stretched the truth. Windschuttle put it beautifully:

> Instead of the mythical tales which all human cultures had used to affirm their sense of self-worth and their place in cosmos, the Greek historians decided to try to record the truth about the past. They did this even though they knew their stories would expose how fragile was their existence, how their heroes could not guarantee their victories, how their oracles could not foretell their future and how their gods could not ensure their fortunes. The essence of history has continued to be that it should try to tell the truth, to describe as best as possible what really happened.
>
> This is no longer the case. The newly dominant theorists within the humanities and social sciences assert that it is impossible to tell the truth about the past or to use history to produce knowledge in any objective sense at all.[62]

Thus, universities like Stanford replaced Western Civilization with Culture, Ideas and Values, a course that could part with Dante, Aquinas, Locke, Thomas More, Virgil, Cicero, Tacitus and Galileo in favor of names like Karl Marx, Zora Neale Hurston and Sandra Cisneros. Plato's *Republic* is abandoned for kowtowing to "anti-assimilationist movements," complained George Roche, in favor of books like *The Wretched of the Earth* by Frantz Fanon.

In other words, said George Roche, "three thousand years

of our Greek, Roman, Judaic and Christian heritage are simply thrown out, at a faculty meeting, in favor of a purely leftist agenda."[63] The Hillsdale president drew a big laugh from conservative audiences when he suggested the slogan for this reform movement could well be "Hey, Hey, Ho Ho, Western Civ Has Got To Go."

At fundraising events, Dr. Roche suggested no campus in America was safe from the politically correct truth squads. For those who really wanted to lose sleep, he offered the example of an outspoken Louis Farrakhan spokesperson going after Christianity's main man at a University of North Carolina Black Student Movement rally. "We are tired of a blond-haired, pale-skinned, blue-eyed, buttermilk complexioned cracker Christ or peckerwood Jesus," complained this radical speaker, who also dismissed Socrates incorrectly as a short "faggot."[64]

How could Hillsdale screen out this kind of nonsense? Campus rules and regulations that banned, for example, bullhorns, loudspeakers, radio or any other type of audio equipment to encourage assembly for purposes of demonstrations were one answer.[65] When renegade students decided to tar and feather the bronze eagle at the school's entryway (one of many eagles donated by an important Hillsdale patron), the school's no-knock policy allegedly went into high gear. Suspects were reportedly awakened in the middle of the night and rousted out of bed in their jammies for interrogation. And when outsiders threatened to heckle a speaker like Alexander Haig over the issue of American intervention in El Salvador, Central Hall came up with a great way to keep the peace. The administrators were not about to let these dissidents, who had assaulted Haig with fruit during another Michigan campus appearance, cause trouble at Hillsdale. To avoid a repeat performance, the administration asked the football team to don jackets and ties, and surround the campus 40 feet apart. "Sure enough," vice president Ron Trowbridge explained, "the El Salvador kids showed up on the other side of the street." But none of them crossed Hillsdale's line of scrimmage.[66] Haig's lecture went off without a hitch.

And that was the beauty of Hillsdale. Parents could rest easy knowing that nothing would interfere with educating their children in the Western tradition. "Thank you for entrusting your children to our care," the president told the teary-eyed moms and dads as they hugged their freshman sons and daughters goodbye at the dorms each fall. As the parents drove back home through nearby villages like Jonesville and Moscow, Roche's reassuring words were ringing in their ears. "We will do our best to keep them on the path that you have so carefully and lovingly constructed."[67]

This approach was lauded by reporters from papers like the *Detroit News,* which asked, "What do other colleges have that Hillsdale College doesn't? Oh, things like hippies, beatniks, radicals, picket lines, teach-ins, riots, marijuana, LSD and federal aid. Its students believe a lot of things their parents believe and don't form up at the drop of a hat to protest some 'social injustice.'"[68]

At parents' weekends, mom and dad could have a look for themselves. Joining one of these events in the Spring of 2000, I found the entire faculty neatly arranged at long folding tables. The scene was reminiscent of grade school parent-teacher conferences. It was here that parents had an opportunity to meet with every one of their child's professors. It was a wonderful opportunity for parents and teachers to share information that might help improve their son or daughter's education. Bravo, Hillsdale.

A class act, this was the moment where parents met leading lights of the Hillsdale faculty such as political science professor Mickey Craig. With all the attention focused on Title IX and fundraising, protest demonstrations and *in loco parentis*, it was easy to lose sight of what Hillsdale really stood for. Listening to Mickey Craig lecture on Socrates was an honor and if you listened closely, the experience could even change your life.

For a man who never wrote a single word, Socrates certainly had legs. Fortunately Plato came to the rescue, immortalizing the Greek philosopher's wisdom in *The Republic*. Socrates wasn't just ahead of his time, he was ahead of our time. Professors like Craig loved teaching him because he asked questions that are as pertinent to our future as they were to his own.

Like Christ and Moses, Socrates wanted little for himself. He was hardly a role model. "In fact," Craig said, "he was actually a kind of deadbeat dad, not much of a breadwinner." Nagged by his wife for his inability to earn a decent living, he wasn't concerned with personal power. He remained objective about those who were.

"Socrates believed that politics is distinguished from tyranny by the fact that the authority in the regime is not based on coercion. It's based on a partnership. You are an equal citizen participating in making laws that govern your relationship. A ruler is a person who makes laws in deliberation with others.

"All of this preceded Locke's argument that no one is obligated to follow the rules until they become part of the social contract. Once you join civil society you have obligated yourself. You will pay taxes whether you agree with them or not. If you don't, you will be punished."[69]

Plato's *Republic* underscored this view with the story of

Gyges, a shepherd in the service of the king of Lydia. The issue was framed for Socrates by a student named Glaucon. Following an earthquake, Gyges descended into a rift zone and discovered a corpse wearing nothing but a gold ring. Gyges took the ring and then returned to meet his fellow shepherds. At this session, where shepherds were compiling their monthly sheep audit for the king, Gyges made a remarkable discovery. By reversing the ring, he became invisible. Amazed by the fact that the other shepherds spoke of him as if he weren't there, he restored the ring to its original position and reappeared.

Sensing a great opportunity, Gyges lobbied to be one of the messengers to the king. At the court he seduced the queen, then persuaded her to help him murder the king and take control of the kingdom. This raised a question that resonated through the pages of *The Republic:* How would people behave if they knew they weren't going to get caught?

Given such a magic ring, Glaucon had a hard time believing that any man "can be imagined to be of such an iron nature that he would stand fast in justice. No man would keep his hands off what was not his own when he could safely take what he liked out of the market or go into houses and lie with any one at his pleasure, or kill or release from prison whom he would, and in all respects be like a God among men.... Thus we may truly affirm to be a great proof that a man is just, not willingly or because he thinks that justice is any good to him individually, but of necessity, for wherever any one thinks that he can safely be unjust, there he is unjust. For all men believe in their hearts that injustice is far more profitable to the individual than justice.

"If you could imagine anyone obtaining this power of becoming invisible, and never doing any wrong or touching what was another's, he would be thought by the lookers-on to be a most wretched idiot, although they would praise him to one another's faces, and keep up appearances with one another from a fear that they too might suffer injustice."[70]

For Craig the "Gyges argument made by Glaucon is that the best way of life by nature is to be perfectly selfish, to be a tyrant using the whole city for personal pleasure. If every human can be invisible, all of us can be tyrants."

Glaucon asked Socrates to refute this argument. His response, says Craig, is based on the concept that "justice is not natural. Justice is a compact between people who wish they could be tyrants but don't have the talent. Since people didn't want to live under a tyrant, they got together to avoid suffering."[71]

Epiphanies such as these had been the heart and soul of life at Hillsdale for over 150 years. In a quiet way they reflected the real power of the academy hidden behind the spotlight trained on the school's David and Goliath battle with Washington, D.C. What the Hillsdales of America offered young people was not just a meal ticket but a chance to develop the moral framework that would help them achieve what Socrates called the "natural right." As Craig explained it, "The worst thing is to be a tyrant because you destroy your own soul."

Part of this message was carried forward by Roche's dearly loved author, J. R. R. Tolkein. Reading aloud to his children from *The Hobbit* and *The Lord of the Rings* trilogy at bedtime, the president brought Middle Earth to the Middle West in an unforgettable manner. This book was the fruit of Tolkein's extraordinary erudition. Here the ring of power, like the ring of Gyges, makes its wearer invisible. Indeed, early in the story, Gollum finds the ring and his wife demands it for a birthday present. The battle ends when Gollum kills his wife. Later in the story, a hobbit named Bilbo discovers the ring of power in a mine where goblins live. Its rightful owner, wretch of the earth Gollum, tries to murder the hobbit and steal back his lost ring. But in the nick of time, Bilbo discovers that slipping on the ring makes him invisible.

This dramatic escape sets the scene for a famous story of temptation, corruption and the seduction of power pitting the little hobbits against the dark lord Sauron. The mortal men who accepted rings of power from the dark lords were enslaved and turned into ghosts. All of the really good people in *The Hobbit* and *The Lord of the Rings* know that they cannot wear the ring of power because it will corrupt them no matter how good they are. At one point little Frodo, who is trying to give away a ring that will carry its wearer to destruction, offers it to one of the great Elf Queens. She lets him see a vision of the tragedy awaiting her if she wears the ring. She would suddenly have all the worst aspects of the dark lord.

As a result, all the Hobbits know that they must throw the ring into the volcano, Mt. Doom, if they wish to see the light of day. Unless the ring is destroyed, the dark lord Sauron will use it to gain control of the world. Roche loved this story so much that casual references to Tolkein popped up in conversation. Describing his Hillsdale team as the "company of the rings," he even brought Tolkein's imagery to Central Hall. Visitors to the president's office noted that at times all that appeared on his beautiful desk were a banker's lamp and Lord of the Rings figurines.

A Socratic campus run by a president who loved Tolkein, Hillsdale was, even to its critics, an extraordinary place. People like former economics professor Anderson professed admiration for "the uniqueness of Hillsdale College, where a personal and close contact exists between faculty and students."[72] Professors didn't just go to class, they pastored churches and offered free counseling services, they gave up weekends to meet with parents and stood up to students when they were wrong, proof positive that academic standards were not being watered down.

There was no grade inflation at Hillsdale. Kay Cosgrove, who flunked Roche's son IV in English because he failed to show for a number of classes, never heard a word of complaint from his father about it. "I liked IV," she said years later, "but he wasn't doing the work."[73] Even though she was the only professor to ever fail IV, her career continued at Hillsdale, where she served her last 16 years on campus as registrar.

Like Craig, Reist and so many other Hillsdale leaders, Kay Cosgrove represented the liberating influence of this liberal arts school. The president had assembled such an impressive faculty and raised so much money that it was easy for the board of trustees to overlook some of the bad vibrations emanating from the House of Roche.

One part of the story was the worst-kept secret in town, the crumbling marriage of George and June Roche. On the road they were a magnificent couple. Together they raised so much money that even after nearly three decades of tireless effort, Roche couldn't quantify the total. "We raised over 300 million dollars," he would explain at the end of his reign. "But there was another large pot of money out there we never did count." The balance, as much as $200 million, was in wills and estates that were not always formally pledged. "A 77-year-old *Imprimis* reader from Kansas leaves money in a trust, that we didn't know, " he explained. This kind of found money was Hillsdale's legacy and it reflected the phenomenal success of the Roches and a fundraising team led by the school's development director, John Cervini.

Accumulating over 3 million air miles, President Roche

worked the conservative community brilliantly. Accompanied by wife June, who was convinced she acquired an autoimmune disease from breathing too much foul airplane air, Roche laughed off the advice of would-be fundraising consultants who insisted he was doing it all wrong.

"We didn't use a fundraising operation," he explained. "I advanced a position with *Imprimis*. We had a huge untapped resource, hundreds of thousands of people who knew us through our publication. At parties or receptions we could develop a relationship, that's what development was about. We talked about the school and if there was a proposal they might be interested in we would let them know. The professional fundraising consultants thought we didn't know what we were doing. They wanted us to use the 'Huns are at the door approach,' crying that if we didn't get money we'd close in 15 minutes. We'd say thanks and come back in 50 years."

Perhaps the most extraordinary aspect of Hillsdale's fundraising apparatchiks was the way they lured in huge donations from people who knew little of the campus or its students. This was a tradition that dated back to the college's earliest days. Hillsdale missionaries such as Dunn were raising consciousness as well as money. At every stop along the way they converted audiences to the Freewill Baptist's antislavery platform.

Dunn was not just building a college he would ultimately lead, he was creating the constituency that would elect Abraham Lincoln and ultimately free the slaves. His rural church audiences were impressed by the fact that Dunn saw Hillsdale College as a humanitarian beacon for the region destined to become America's Heartland. Many would never forget his words of inspiration that set them on the path of righteousness.

"Do you remember that night in 1853 when you spoke at a schoolhouse near my father's residence in Illinois?" asked

Judge Hoke, who went on to become the American consul to Nova Scotia. "Your burning eloquence and strong language are still vivid in my memory. No photograph could retain more distinctly the scene than my mind now holds it. The benches, the tallow candles, the desk you stood behind, the green glasses you wore, the gestures you made, the packed audience that leaned forward to catch every word that fell from your lips, are clearer than any other scene of my early life. The whole nation was then proslavery. It was very unpopular for you to make that speech at that time in Illinois. Indeed, I think the whole antislavery party was mostly composed of Freewill Baptists, Quakers and Oberlin College. I was attending school where the faculty, all Methodist preachers, denounced the agitation of the slavery question. My father, who had heard you before, drove seven miles to the seminary and back that night, that I, a youth of 17, should hear that speech. It is not strange that when I learned of Hillsdale College and that you were to be one of the faculty I determined to go to this Christian and antislavery college."[74]

But as the school traded on Dunn's legacy, conflicts of interest were inevitable. In some cases deals were cut at the highest level without considering potential adverse consequences. Among the most astonished faculty members was a professor of classical literature and ancient history named Michael Poliakoff. Educated at Yale, Oxford and the University of Michigan, he was given a warm welcome by his Christian colleagues when he arrived on campus in 1987.

One of the few Jews in Hillsdale, Poliakoff welcomed many faculty friends into his kosher home and loved teaching and working with the college's excellent students. When he broke his leg, a physical therapist named IV did a great job helping him recuperate. The new professor enjoyed listening to IV's father articulate his vision, particularly when he pointed out that "Hillsdale welcomed Afro-Americans and women onto the campus long before the federal government thought this was the right thing to do."[75]

But one day Poliakoff was presented a book called *The Talmud Unmasked* by a colleague who suggested that he sit down and read it. When he learned that this anti-Semitic literature had come from Hillsdale's Mossey Library, Poliakoff immediately took the matter to Dean of Faculty John Reist. Equally surprised, Reist discussed the problem with President Roche and Mossey Library director Dan Joldersma.

The book had come from a closet-sized room in the library basement that contained some of the worst hate literature Poliakoff had ever seen. In addition to *The Talmud Unmasked,* the translation of a Russian blood libel and *The Protocols of the Elders of Zion,* the collection also included a title called *The Original Mr. Jew* and demeaning periodicals attacking blacks and Jews.

The book that leaked out of the locked room was part of the Grieb Collection, research documents donated along with a six-figure stock gift to the school. Normally collections of this kind found in great European libraries are made available to scholars studying the Holocaust. But the Hillsdale collection was never even accessioned or cataloged. The fact that even the dean of faculty didn't know of the Grieb collection implied that these anti-Semitic books and papers were simply being stored in secrecy. Dr. Reist, who almost became physically ill over this collection of racist research documents said they would have to go. Library director Dan Joldersma wisely suggested the Holocaust research library at the Simon Wiesenthal Center in Los Angeles.

Locking the papers was certainly the prudent thing to do.

But how had one faculty member with an apparent interest in anti-Semitic literature breached the locked room? And, asked Dr. Poliakoff, why was there no apology forthcoming from Roche?

"The answer I wanted was *Ashamnu,* the Yom Kippur repetition of the public confessions of sin. I would have much preferred hearing, 'We made a real mistake,' even if that stock was worth $10 million. I cannot tell you in all candor what would have happened if the stock had held its value or increased. Why wasn't it being housed off campus in a triple locked storeroom, or quite frankly why was it ever taken in the first place?

"My guess is from the way this thing was structured, presumably no one ever thought there would ever be any accountability.... My guess was that the overwhelming majority of faculty never had a clue." Poliakoff deplored the compromise decision to house the papers in a locked room. He believed the college should have said, "If you want to give us this stuff it is only going to be in a special collection where we admit special students of hate literature and we will only allow it to be seen as intellectual pornography."

Although the locked room mystery was never solved, the controversial research collection was quietly moved out of town to the Wiesenthal Center with the kind of security one might expect for spent fuel rods from a nuclear reactor.

Harder to hide at this time was the Roche soap opera beginning to play out at impromptu venues across town. From pizza delivery drivers to local ministers, the first family's problem became a popular topic of discussion. Disgruntled faculty, overworked students, underpaid staff, just about anyone who had a gripe with the college, traded rumor and innuendo about the Broadlawn bunch. Like the Kennedys and the Clintons, the Roches found that their success inspired a gossip mill that resembled the headlines found on supermarket tabloids in the checkout line at Kroger. There were times when the ghostly figure of George Roche stumbling down the street from a combination of diabetes complications and vision problems prompted his closest friends to wonder if he was on the verge of retirement.

"George was a sick man who pushed himself unmercifully," said his wife June. "He would cut short vacations to go back to work. He was addicted to his work and he had a strong sense of obligation. The problem was he always wanted to do too much.

"Childhood-onset diabetes is something that gets worse as you get older. It's more serious than adult-onset diabetes. He was frequently sick with insulin reactions and would get disoriented."[76]

The president tried to fend off his illness by popping glucose tablets he kept in his pockets. But when these tablets failed to work, his blood sugar level dropped dangerously low, and he began to hallucinate and in some cases, black out. Sometimes this malady struck while he was on the road at places like Clare Boothe Luce's home in Hawaii or visiting Piccadilly Circus in London. On one occasion he was walking to a New York meeting with CBS News executive and college board member Frank Shakespeare when he collapsed. He was rushed by ambulance to a West Side hospital and never made it to the meeting. Diabetes also led to a serious vision problem. At one point in the mid-'90s the president nearly went blind. After a year of failing vision, laser surgery restored his sight.[77]

Social drinking compounded his difficulties. A lusty man who wrote novels romanticizing serious drinkers in the wilds of Colorado, Roche's big problem was the fact that diabetes made it hard for him to handle alcohol. The fact that he drank when he knew he shouldn't, added to his difficulties at home. Scenes between George and June Roche were so common that people asked not to be seated next to the couple at public functions. Reist, a professor of Christianity and literature and pastor of Somerset Congregational Church, told of how his sister, in town for a party, asked the identity of a couple arguing in the driveway.

"I just witnessed the worst case of spousal abuse I've ever seen in my life," she told her brother. "That's our president and his wife," the professor told her.[78]

In June Roche's mind, her husband's shouting mirrored his health problem. She found the diabetes made him "very nervous and shaky. If you walked up behind him in the bathroom he would jump out of his skin. It actually got to the point where he developed diabetic neuropathy, he had no feeling in his feet. If you can't feel your feet, what is going on in your head?"

For Lissa Roche, some of these health problems were reminiscent of her own family. As a child she watched doctors treat her mother Charlotte for rheumatoid arthritis with medications that led to distinct personality changes. And when June Roche's physician put her on steroids to combat an autoimmune disease, Hillsdale's first lady became surprisingly aggressive. After telling her husband off emphatically she decided that the medication was part of the problem and quit the drug.

"Even if we weren't getting along well, we were working to get along as a family. I worked to keep everyone together and keep everyone in tow. I thought it was important to him. It was important to him up to a point and then everything went haywire.

"What we do know is that there was an emotional relationship (with Lissa) that was too deep and as the older person he should have recognized what the pitfalls were. He recognized that he should have sent them (IV and Lissa) away and done something to remedy the situation. He should have handled this years ago. When you are a teacher you deal with a girl student who has a crush on you. You should be able to deal with it. It is important that you should keep work separate from family."[79]

As the marriage deteriorated, George spent more time hanging out with friends in a two-car garage behind Broadlawn, where he worked on old vehicles and stored his guns. It was here that the men hung out after handball or a sporting event, enjoying a beer and shooting the breeze. IV would come around with George V who brought along college friends surprised to find themselves having a drink with the leader of a school that strictly enforced a no-keg policy.

One of the few schools in the country that could proudly boast that its student regulations had tightened up in recent years, Hillsdale did not allow parties on school nights, banned overnight visits in dorm rooms (a policy enforced with random bed checks) and, perhaps most significantly in the AIDS era, did not supply condoms through the student health service. Like some Catholic colleges, Hillsdale was a school where the rhythm method lived.

The contradictions frequently discussed by the school's critics were part of what made Hillsdale unique. In Roche's republic, minority points of view didn't last. And when his enemies suggested this was unfair, the president liked to quote Henry Kissinger: "In faculty politics the stakes are so low." What really mattered was the fact that the president was having a good time.

"I always enjoyed what I was doing," said Hillsdale's CEO with the boyish enthusiasm that made him the Gordie Howe of college presidents, skating along effortlessly like the former Detroit and Houston hockey star long after contemporaries had claimed their retirement gifts. And like Howe, he was proud to have a son on the team. "There are very few places where you have the opportunity to say things that don't go with the common flow," Roche explained.

This heterodoxy was, in many ways, inconsistent with the school's founding fathers. "The Freewill Baptists," said Roche, "had less zest for operations than for founding. If they had been running Hillsdale College, I couldn't have come." The secularization of Hillsdale, at the expense of its church affiliation, was critical to its success. "We were independent of the college's past history. We determined the issues for our audience. That small "c" Catholicity was important for my peace of mind."

This approach meant that many "non-denominational people came to Hillsdale and found what they were looking for. We often thought that if we had all the people who found what they were looking for at Hillsdale there would probably have been a riot."[80]

Heading off that riot was no easy task. Scholars like Rev. James Burtchaell, former provost at Notre Dame, suggested in his book *The Dying of the Light* that secularization of Christian colleges was a tricky business. In the process of broadening their reach to attract affluent donors and corporate support, these schools were forced to diminish the spiritual ties that were an important part of their birthright. Was it possible that this shift away from the church was a Faustian bargain?

At Hillsdale one test came when President Nixon's former special counsel, Charles Colson, delivered a Dostoevskian speech called "Can man be good without God?" Director of a prison ministry, Colson mentioned Jesus twice in his remarks. But when the edited version of his remarks came back from *Imprimis*'s Lissa Roche, Christ had ended up on the cutting room floor. She explained that school rules prevented "use of the Lord's name in any of their publications." In a rare veto of his daughter-in-law, George Roche restored the cuts at Colson's request.[81]

Crises of this kind were rare, because few *Imprimis* contributors mentioned Jesus in their articles. Lissa's editing was widely appreciated. Some bestselling authors like Michael Medved, even hired her to do freelance research on such books as *Hollywood vs. America*. She also assisted Medved's wife on an anti-divorce book. A great researcher, Lissa was particularly adept at digging out factoids that documented the conservative mantra. The results were easy to spot in her carefully crafted editing of Roche's books and writing in *Imprimis*.

FDR's New Deal was really a "pretext for massive collectivization of American society throughout the decade of the 1930s." Dwight D. Eisenhower "proved ... that Republican administrations usually ratify, then reverse the collectivist inroads of their Democratic predecessors." Even Ronald Reagan, who appointed Roche to chair his Council on Educational Research, proved to be a disappointment. "Whatever one thought of Reagan's actual accomplishments, it was uncertain whether much had changed."[82]

This brand of pessimism, voiced by Roche after quitting his job as chair of Reagan's Council on Educational Research, characterized Hillsdale's world view and the president's collaboration with his daughter-in-law. He was quick and funny. She was the fellow traveler who polished his prose, making him sound like Paul Harvey at a commencement. In the land of the politically blindsided, the one-liner was king.

As underdogs challenging the comfortable assumptions of statism, George and Lissa Roche attracted iconoclasts from across the land. Among them was Reist.

"I'm a capitalist, but I don't think Jesus struggled and writhed on the cross so that you and I could have big bank accounts," he told the president. "Capitalism needs prophetic judgment as much as Marxism."

Bemused by the fact that Roche wrote a book attacking the high salaries of faculty when he was earning more than $500,000 a year, Reist compared Roche with the Greek sophists who "tried to put people asleep by an effective rhetoric that said 'Buy a Buick,' 'Vote Democratic' or 'This Bud's For You.' Anyone who challenged that rhetoric," claimed Reist, "was a candidate for censure."

"I was in a meeting where George said, 'Do you actually think faculty has freedom to ask these questions?' I said we not only ought to tolerate it, we ought to be encouraging it."

The president's outbursts mirrored some of his unhappiness at home. He needed the thick skin of an armadillo to survive his critics who dogged him from Central Hall to Broadlawn. George's leading ally was Lissa Roche, who urged him to leave one of his worst critics, his wife June.

In many ways the problems plaguing the Roches mirrored some of the debates that animated the classroom. Family showdowns took place at Broadlawn, the stone cottage shared by IV and Lissa, in driveways and bedrooms, at dinner parties and even hospital rooms. Some of the issues such as homework or relocating to John Denver country might have not seemed worthy of a therapist's couch. But collectively they touched all the causes that sparked public demonstrations on politically correct campuses: feminism, education policy, family values and most certainly human rights. Another problem was that Roche's relationship with his daughter-in-law stretched the boundaries of common sense. As political science professor Craig put it: "Lissa admired him and he encouraged that admiration.... He encouraged the kind of blind loyalty that was very unhealthy.

"Aristotle said politics is about more than government. For Aristotle politics includes all partnerships beginning with the family. (Find a) proper way to treat your wife and a healthy city will result. Aristotle also said a good leader is happy to have people who aren't cowards and will look him in the eye and say, 'That is wrong.' I say to myself, I should have said to George, 'Lissa shouldn't admire you so much or IV should go off and teach somewhere else.' But I didn't do that."[83]

For Craig, one of IV's closest friends, this problem mirrored some of the difficulties he experienced as divisional dean of social science. A turning point came when he brought in an exciting professor for the education department named John Finnell. Willing to take a $50,000 pay cut from an industry job, Finnell team-taught a course on educational and political theory.[84] For reasons Craig could never understand, Finnell, one of the best professors Hillsdale ever hired, never received mandatory staff evaluations of his work. After Finnell was let go, he quickly landed a six-figure job in the software industry. The decision not to rehire Finnell demonstrated the challenge of middle management in an autocracy. Convinced that it would be impossible to continue serving as an effective administrator, Craig returned full time to the classroom. "I decided they let me teach what I teach and that's a lot to be thankful for," he said. "I get to set my own course."[85]

Some who confronted Roche on issues of this kind came

away quoting the words of Lord Acton: "Power tends to corrupt and absolute power corrupts absolutely." This view, which Roche liked to cite in his own books attacking federal education policy, reflected the bitterness of faculty who saw Roche as a Machiavellian-style prince. For the president, who sat in his Central Hall office, moving around his desktop figurines from Tolkein's *Lord of the Rings* trilogy, the backlash was inevitable. "In a quarter of a century of doing something you make waves and get a little brine in people's eyes. They don't like it and you better have a thick skin." But even those closest to the college leader began having second thoughts about his stewardship.

His wife, eldest son and daughter-in-law were convinced, for different reasons, that their interests and those of the college were not served by his continued leadership. Faculty members and some students also began asking questions that added to the confusion and uncertainty. The more successful Hillsdale became, the harder it was to reconcile the school's public image with Roche's private life. Predictably, it was George and June Roche's marriage that disintegrated first in ways that left some faculty members calling for his resignation.

This was not just the Christian Coalition talking. Catholics, Jews, agnostics and even atheists were concerned about the battles at Broadlawn. Their fear was that without June's stabilizing influence, George would be unable to manage his job or his family. During the last three years of their marriage she had traveled with him constantly, always at the ready in case he went into insulin shock. Without June, who could possibly step in to help him raise young Jake? What about his ailing mother, "Granaw" Margaret? There were rumors that IV and Lissa were struggling too. Who could possibly run Broadlawn and provide that vital domestic touch that was part and parcel of the Hillsdale family at Homecoming, graduation, Freedom Quest-style fundraisers and a myriad of other events that helped secure Hillsdale's place on the honor roll of liberal arts education?

Like many episodes in the life of Hillsdale's first family, Roche's decision to leave his wife was a family affair. In July 1997 he took a month-long vacation in Hawaii with June, IV, Lissa, his son Jake and daughter Maggie. For the president, who had so many frequent flyer miles he liked to joke that Northwest Airlines owed him an airplane, this kind of getaway was easy to arrange. Except for an occasional stag retreat at the Bohemian Grove in California, Hillsdale's president made it a point to always vacation with his family. After selling one beloved family retreat in Montana south of Glacier Park, the president bought a hunting lodge on the Snake River Canyon south of Jackson Hole, Wyoming.

Closer to home, they also enjoyed many getaways at a northern Michigan A-frame cottage near Gaylord. The dream of retiring to a home on the range with the entire family was now beginning to crumble. June believed that Lissa was secretly devoting part of her Hawaii vacation to helping George plan his divorce.

George decided to break the bad news on a Saturday in August 1998. Interrupting a luncheon he asked June to join him upstairs. "I've taken all the money out of the bank and canceled all the credit cards," he told her. "Here's a check for $1,000 to tide you over. Don't worry. You'll be well taken care of."[86] In the divorce complaint drawn up by a Hillsdale attorney, June's occupation was listed as "domestic engineer." After threatening her with eviction from Broadlawn, George asked for full custody of Jake. Scouting for an attorney in the Detroit area, June was discouraged to discover that a number were reluctant to help her take on the Hillsdale president. The couple finally decided to put the matter in the capable hands of reasonably priced attorneys in Jackson. They settled the matter with a reasonable alimony and joint custody agreement.

The Roche divorce was final in April 1999. Three months later, June set out with Jake for Buena Vista, Colorado, where they planned to spend a month at a cabin she had rented for $1,000. Their journey west was interrupted in St. Louis where Jake was hospitalized with food poisoning. In Hays, Kansas, June needed medical attention for a gall bladder attack. They continued on to Buena Vista, and after one day at the cabin, they headed down to Denver Lutheran Hospital, where surgeons removed her gall bladder. Doctors told June a CAT scan showed signs of cancer later confirmed by a biopsy. Back home at the University of Michigan hospital in Ann Arbor, doctors diagnosed Hodgkin's lymphoma.[87]

The fact that June's treatment began shortly after the divorce was finalized compounded ill feelings toward George among some faculty members who blamed the president for the breakup of his marriage.

While June's friends drove her to Ann Arbor for chemotherapy treatments, she was beginning to settle in a New Orleans-style home on Broad Street in Hillsdale. Daughter Muriel lived with her husband in a small back unit, while Jake had a room upstairs. Meanwhile, back at Broadlawn, IV and Lissa discovered cleaning house was more difficult than they imagined.

Assuming many of the duties of Hillsdale's first lady, Lissa began redecorating and disposing of surplus property. Some of June's cherished possessions, such as her commemorative medal from the Margaret Thatcher dinner, were handled badly. After snatching this treasure from the trash before the garbage collectors swept it off to the dump, June had to bring in her attorney to make sure other heirlooms didn't end up at the flea market.[88]

While Lissa and IV enjoyed some aspects of life at Broadlawn, this was hardly a plantation lifestyle with mint juleps on the patio and minstrels strumming away on their banjos. When George's diabetes worsened, June had been forced to travel with him constantly. Now this duty was handed over to IV and Lissa. They also cared for Granaw, who had medical problems of her own. The result was sleep deprivation.

"They couldn't sleep with their bedroom door closed," said June, "because if George was wandering around with an insulin reaction, they had to check his skin to see if he was in insulin shock. Similarly if they found Granaw on the floor, IV had to help pick her up and put her back in bed."[89]

Campus historian and neighbor Arlan Gilbert, who had shared a fence with the Roches from the day they moved into Broadlawn, believed IV and Lissa had now come full circle. "This was the house where he lived as a teenager. I remember him playing ball in the backyard. It was the house where he and Lissa dated. There were lots of memories here. In a short time they had gone from an apartment next door over the health center, to the crowded cottage, to the mansion."[90]

While it was still true that IV and Lissa couldn't put together enough money for a home down payment, they were now managing the biggest house in town. Their extended family included IV's brother Jake who was having trouble concentrating on his studies. Lissa, who was already preoccupied with their own son's shaky academic performance and drinking problems, saw Jake as part of her Broadlawn mission statement. Determined to intervene before his grades bottomed out, she suggested that he be sent off to her floating Florida alma mater, now called the Argo Academy. When June said no, Lissa responding by assuming the responsibilities of a case worker, checking in daily with Jake's teachers at the Hillsdale Academy, tutoring him intensively and, during the time he was living with his father, adopting a kind of educational version of tough love. She insisted that if he failed to bring an assignment with him to class, he could not return home to retrieve it.

One morning June broke this edict by driving her son over to Broadlawn where a housekeeper obligingly fetched his forgotten homework. That night, when June brought Jake home to the mansion, Lissa was standing in the driveway yelling, "You can't do that, June. I'm trying to teach him discipline."[91]

Lissa was equally upset with the academic performance of her own son, George V. Critical of the way he was partying with his fraternity friends, upset about his drinking and his inability to pull himself out of academic probation that could lead to expulsion, she confronted George V again and again. Feeling humiliated after one showdown in the driveway, she confided to friends: "I think I've lost him."[92]

Overworked and despondent about her son, Lissa appeared to be losing her famous sense of humor. When she and IV did arrive together for major events, their appearance came as a bit of a surprise. Only after pressure from June did IV and Lissa agree to attend the funeral services for Phillips, the one-time Hillsdale president. "They showed up in street clothes and looked like beatniks," recalled Gilbert.[93]

When Lissa said out loud, "I wish we could get away from here," friends like Gilbert were sympathetic. After a popular Hillsdale College psychology professor, Chris Tsao, divorced his wife, a lecturer in Japanese named Akiko Tani, IV began second-guessing Tsao's decision. The more he joked about Tani's desirability, the angrier Lissa became. When friends reported that Tani was making repeated visits to IV's office at the George Roche Education and Sports Complex, she began wondering if her husband really was just kidding around.[94]

Lissa was also squabbling with June Roche, who was having self-esteem problems of her own. Hillsdale's former first lady was smarting over Central Hall's instructions to keep her distance from college patrons. "I was told I couldn't talk to donors," she said. "I was never thanked for what I did to hold my family together."[95]

For June Roche, who had been a critical part of the Hillsdale family, nursing her husband through so many health crises, keeping donors fed and watered, making sure that Broadlawn represented the family values so critical to the college's mission statement, retirement was difficult. Great at raising money, June had more than one green thumb. After years of planting cuttings taken from the yards of buildings being demolished, she had turned Broadlawn's backyard into a botanical garden. One step ahead of the bulldozers, she even saved cuttings from the infamous Phi Sigma Kappa house, torn down following suspension for a series of problems including social misconduct and poor academic performance.

Now living less than a mile away in a lovely brick home, she was eager to plant some of the 25 varieties of peonies lovingly grown from seed at Broadlawn. It was a great way to keep her mind off chemotherapy. Unfortunately she was not allowed to take any starts from the mansion's backyard because they were campus property. "I had to plant peonies from Wal-Mart."

"Hello, This Is George Roche.
My Wife Just Shot Herself."

I N ITS 150 YEARS HILLSDALE COLLEGE had burned down and been rebuilt, been plucked from the maw of bankruptcy by a local druggist and survived faculty attempts to unionize. But on September 8, 1999, the college was blindsided by an unprecedented personnel crisis. On that day Hillsdale lost the managing editor of the College Press, helmswoman of its leading fundraising tool, the 900,000 circulation magazine *Imprimis*, and George Roche's leading editor and most important ghostwriter. On her last day as she prepared to leave her job, her husband and the state of Michigan, Lissa Roche took care of final details in a note to her staff.

"It grieves me to tell you," Lissa wrote, "that I am unable to continue as managing editor of *Imprimis* and the Hillsdale College Press. I am seeking a divorce from George IV for reasons I can't go into, and it seems best to get out of town immediately. I am sorry to leave you in the lurch like this."[96]

Anticipating campus reaction, Lissa Roche provided the answers that that would have inevitably come up at the champagne-and-punch reception she was eager to avoid. "I know that there will be a lot of talk about my sudden departure; please tell people that although it seems strange that I left in such a secretive manner it was simply to avoid a big fuss. You know me; I hate to be the object of attention. I have been such an object in the college community for many years now. I just want this to be as private as possible, and, most of all, I don't want to have to answer any questions. I will tell you that I am not leaving IV for someone else, since I know that will come up."[97]

In recent months Lissa had been talking with friends about her plans to leave her husband of 22 years. Although their marriage had gone through hard times, this was different. IV had been skipping family vacations and, she felt, he was not giving her the kind of help she sought with their son. Clearly questions about infidelity by her husband had also crossed Lissa's mind. Whether or not her concerns were justified, Lissa believed that this apparent problem was probably beyond her control.

While this was not the first time that IV and Lissa had come close to ending their marriage, each would, in the weeks ahead, have good reason to question the other's fidelity. But nothing in her letter hinted at the larger scandal ahead.

Although some in Hillsdale who had benefited from her labors, such as Professor Gilbert, suspected she may have been underpaid during her 15 years of overachievement at Hillsdale, Lissa made it clear that she did not want a special severance package.[98] She chose to leave no forwarding address, saying, "I will not be reachable by phone or mail. Tell (her colleague) Jill if any job termination paperwork has to be signed or W-2s forwarded later on, please mail to my (twin) sister, Laura Jackson (in Los Angeles). I will not be staying with her, but I will be in touch with her periodically. My final paycheck, if there is one, can be deposited as usual by auto deposit in my joint checking account with IV."

After identifying possible successors at *Imprimis*, she discussed her tendency to heavily edit the work of all contributors. "Remind the new editor that I tended to rewrite almost every *Imprimis* issue from top to bottom, while still trying to retain the unique style of the author. Every sentence needs crafting, sometimes over and over again. I also filled in many missing factual and philosophical points, and did a lot of fact-checking. Many authors are wrong, even about their own bios!"

Handing off the October issue of *Imprimis*, she wrote, "We are very late! I sent the edited version of Steve Forbes remarks to him yesterday and gave him 7 working days to respond. I also gave Ron (Trowbridge) a Margaret Thatcher excerpt to get her approval on during the same period.... Hopefully ... the authors won't have many changes. If Thatcher says no (to the editing), just do a photo section from the last two Shavanos. Be sure to take my name off the copyright section."

Margaret Thatcher

Finally, she added a note about her inability to continue working with author Herbert Swope, the son of a famous New York newspaper publisher, on his autobiography. She asked her colleagues to handle the bad news with grace. "Please send him everything with a note of apology for my being unable to help further: I have resigned, I can't continue for personal reasons, etc."

Lissa intended to send the message to a small list of trusted colleagues. But she accidentally hit a group e-mail button on her Macintosh. In an instant, people across the campus, including many who were not part of her inner circle, were in the know.[99] After accidentally invading her own privacy, she shut down her laptop and began making final arrangements for her leavetaking. At Broadlawn she packed a few clothes into a single bag, jumped in her husband's truck and drove to the Detroit airport. As Lissa's flight took off, her family frantically tried to figure out what to do. She was on her way home to the state that had given America two presidents that loved Hillsdale—Richard M. Nixon and Ronald Reagan.

With Lissa gone, IV could only wait quietly at the stone cottage for divorce papers to be served. And President Roche had lost his most important co-worker and a daughter-in-law he loved very much. The college's development office had lost a colleague whose brilliant editing had made *Imprimis* one of the most powerful fundraising tools in the history of American higher education. Hillsdale College Press authors had lost their guiding light and America's conservative movement was deprived of one of its most enterprising and imaginative editorial voices. And Jake Roche had lost a tutor and fishing buddy. If there were any detractors of Lissa, I couldn't find them.

News that Lissa was leaving IV and abandoning her campus position changed so many Hillsdale lives that it was fortunate she accidentally hit the group e-mail button. At least now everyone knew the truth. A woman who did not give away much, Lissa finally acknowledged the wisdom of friends who believed Hillsdale was hazardous to her health.

If, as Reist suggests, "the college was built to some degree on the shoulders of June Roche," her divorce and the parallel crisis in Lissa's marriage to IV were critical matters to the board of trustees. The apparent disintegration of both marriages was at the center of a drama so complicated that even those closest to the Roches were caught off guard. Gilbert, who was a neighbor and friend of the family, an author who benefited from Lissa Roche's editing and who championed George Roche's leadership, said, "I have worked here for 40 years. Never in my wildest imagination could I imagine this happening."[100]

When Lissa assumed some of the duties of the president's wife she became Hillsdale's first daughter-in-law. As her marriage to IV deteriorated, her bond with her father-in-law deepened. A trophy daughter-in-law, she was so loyal to Roche that it appeared nothing could damage their friendship.

Longtime residents like Melinda Von Sydow, who taught journalism and English at Hillsdale before moving on to a position at the local campus of Jackson Community College, felt as if the entire community was being pulled "through the looking glass." Like Lissa, Von Sydow had come to Hillsdale from California in the 1970s, married and raised a family. "Lissa was sweet and funny but her job was extremely demanding ... she was under a lot of pressure at her job."

As her role changed so did her father-in-law's. "He (George Roche) took family to a new level," said Von Sydow and the result was beginning to look like a "rather Greek tragedy." In the tradition of Hippolytus by Euripides, the campus could "see all the warning signs, people screaming, misplaced loyalty and affection. ... It's profoundly literary. If we learn something from literature it's that people are capable of the most amazing things."

In Greek mythology, Phaedra, the wife of Theseus, falls in love with her stepson Hippolytus. She then falsely accuses Hippolytus of raping her after spurning his advances. Theseus pleads his case with Poseidon, who takes Hippolytus's life. Distraught by this tragedy, Phaedra kills herself. In his play, Euripides suggests that Phaedra's fate is brought on by a series of psychological problems including mistakes in judgment, anger and miscommunication.

In *Hippolytus,* the playwright leaves the issue of guilt and culpability up in the air. It is true that Theseus brings down a curse on Hippolytus. He believed that there was a sexual relationship between Phaedra and her stepson. Whether this actually is true is left open by Euripides and by Racine, who wrote *Phèdre,* a popular French version of the same drama in the seventeenth century.

The foreshadowing that made this play so powerful was less apparent in the House of Roche. Despite her problems at home, Lissa put on a convincing game face, one that persuaded the campus that at heart she remained self-confident, assertive and always frank. One example was an August 1999 garden party in the arboretum. Food, wine and music flowed until 2 A.M. The highlight of this event for the 200 guests was a song performed by the widow of Alex Shtromas, a professor of Eastern European studies. When one guest told Lissa, the belle of the ball, that he was touched by this loving memorial, she said, "Christ, you didn't know Alex."[101]

While Lissa enjoyed much about her new role at Broadlawn, life with father certainly did not do wonders for her marriage to IV. During their time in the mansion, IV complained of stomach problems brought on by stress. Typically this malady seemed to peak just before a family outing. Just as George, Lissa, George V and Jake were piling in the car for a day trip or a weekend getaway, IV would beg off. He'd settle his stomach by staying home. This particular problem tended to always come up at the last minute and turned family vacation plans into a scene from a Chevy Chase movie. One of the worst showdowns took place in July 1999, when George, Lissa, George V and Jake were climbing into the car to drive to see Lissa's sister Linda and her family who lived in the Buffalo area, not far from Niagara Falls. At the last minute, IV decided to drop out of the vacation trip due to another stomach problem. Like a runway in a Greek theater, the family driveway became the scene of yet another showdown. Lissa's outburst didn't help and once again IV was home alone. When she returned, Lissa began listening closely to rumors that her husband was possibly interested in another, very beautiful woman.

As it turned out, IV wasn't the only Roche she was worried about. Unable to track George down on various business trips, she began frantically calling his secretary to learn his whereabouts. At one point, she desperately phoned board of trustees chairman, Don Mossey at 7 A.M. to get a number for her father-in-law. Why was Dr. Roche suddenly out of range?[102]

Her worst fears were realized shortly after fleeing to California in early September 1999. When she called her husband with information on how to retrieve his missing truck in the Detroit Airport parking lot, Lissa learned that Roche had been secretly dating a nurse living in Louisville, Kentucky, named Dean Hagan. The couple had been introduced a year earlier by one of the Hillsdale College trustees. The two had set a wedding date for September 13. Although Lissa had never heard of Roche's fiancée, she was not unknown to the Jackson family. Hagan had once worked for Lissa's father, a surgeon named Jack Jackson, in the operating room of a

Louisville hospital. Hagan and the president had carried on their love affair in secret, using cell phones as a secure communications channel.[103] In Lissa's mind there were apparently two "other women" in her life.

This news should have reaffirmed her decision to leave Hillsdale. Suspicious of her husband and now virtually certain that there was no chance of reuniting the extended family high in the Rockies, California was looking better by the minute. However, instead of heading for her sister Laura's home, she immediately decided to book a return flight to Michigan. IV was spared a journey to the Detroit airport to retrieve his truck.

The following day, September 9, 1999, began with a crisis at June Roche's home on Broad Street. After returning home from chemotherapy in Ann Arbor, she learned that her daughter Muriel, already ailing from the flu and adrenal failure, had been taken to the emergency room with an infection of the heart. As she was leaving to care for Muriel, her daughter Maggie called to announce she was driving down from Hastings, two hours away. Unaware of Lissa's decision to fly home, she wanted to help IV out in the wake of his wife's disappearance.

On the way to the hospital, June stopped at Broadlawn to give the key to a housekeeper who would keep an eye on the family dog at the Broad Street home. Her ex-husband greeted her at the door, announcing, in the midst of these crises, that he had set a wedding date with Dean.[104]

When Lissa Roche returned to Hillsdale in IV's truck, she learned that Muriel was beginning to recover. With this crisis now under control, she turned her energy to Broadlawn. While most of the campus was preoccupied with Homecoming weekend, Lissa and IV were at a crossroads. Lissa, who had already announced she was leaving IV, was forced to make a difficult decision. If she moved out of Broadlawn and did not return to the stone cottage with her husband, Lissa would be abandoning all hope of rebuilding her family. Hedging her bets, she decided to move back in with IV at the stone cottage and try to retake Broadlawn.

The argument she was framing suggested that her father-in-law's remarriage would destroy the extended family, hurting George V and Jake, who were still recovering from the impact of George's divorce from June. Her logic appeared to be undercut by the fact that she had already announced her own intention to divorce IV. If her husband decided to remain in Hillsdale, perhaps she and her father-in-law could live together with Granaw and Jake in Colorado. The idea sounded a little crazy but it just might give everyone a fresh start. Why, maybe even George V might come along.

Two days after she left her husband, Lissa was back at Broadlawn helping IV collect their belongings and piling them into the back of the same truck she had secretly taken to Detroit. Neighbors like the Gilberts watched the couple move their belongings against the backdrop of Homecoming festivities.

As she carried out her belongings, Lissa spoke at length with George Roche's 56-year-old fiancée. Hagan was standing in the master bathroom upstairs when Lissa suddenly walked in and took a seat on top of the closed commode. Not sure of the significance of her unexpected guest's body language, Hagan sat down on the floor. Lissa launched into an attack on George that sounded like a cross between an Ann Landers column and a *Saturday Night Live* routine. Eager to educate Hagan on what it is like to a marry a Roche, she explained that George was truly a horrible man.

"Lissa," Hagan told her, "if you are that uncomfortable

being in the family, why don't you get out?"

This dialogue continued over the next several days at Broadlawn, with Lissa using the slightest pretext to explain why the Roche-Hagan marriage could never work. She began conversations with suggestions on the best way to carry forward in-progress redecorating with the town's top tradespeople. Then the first daughter-in-law shifted gears and made a strong case against Hagan marrying Roche. Even after her move was over Lissa found excuses to return. On one occasion, she returned some small Broadlawn bathroom canisters carried off by mistake and then led Dean into the sunroom. Lissa ticked off a whole series of reasons to call off the marriage, including George Roche's failing health. "If you only knew what I know, you would leave him," she hinted.

"Lissa," Hagan told her, "I'm not listening to this."[105]

The Roche/Hagan nuptials, held at Trinity Lutheran Church on September 13, were the social event of Hillsdale's fall season. Although a sore throat prevented George's daughter Maggie from singing, Jake made a wonderful altar boy. IV, dressed in a suit, sat with the younger family members while Lissa, wearing a skirt and sweater, remained in the back with Granaw. Hagan was a nervous wreck, half expecting Lissa to rise from her pew when the minister asked if there was anyone in the congregation who knew why the couple should not be joined in holy matrimony. Fortunately, those present all held their peace.

Hagan felt great as she returned to Broadlawn for the reception. But in the midst of the festivities, while mingling with half a dozen guests, the bride felt a tug on her arm. It was Lissa, resuming the dialogue that had begun a few days earlier in the bathroom. This time she traded her careful barbs for language that would make a sailor blush: "I just want you to know, and excuse my French, that you have just married into the most fucked-up family you will ever know."

"Then why don't you get out of the family," Hagan told her in front of the shocked guests. Before Lissa had a chance to answer, Hagan excused herself and walked over to George.[106]

After the wedding Lissa began asserting herself in other ways. Preparing for a dedication ceremony, Roche's secretary, Pat Loper, asked Hagan to come with her to learn how to robe the president and put on his doctoral hood. But before they could adjourn to another room, Lissa turned to her new stepmother and said, "Dean, George is going in with me and sitting with me." Hagan abandoned her robing lesson and after the president was dressed by his secretary, the Roche trio headed into the ceremony together.

At other events Lissa also launched into an impromptu version of "I've Got a Secret." When she, IV, Dean and George took their seats for a campus play, Lissa killed time before the opening curtain by whispering into George's ear for a few minutes and then turning to IV and whispering to him as well. What, Dean wondered to herself, was this all about?

The wedding appeared to bring an end to Lissa's vision of restoring the extended family. She felt particularly bad for Jake and her own son George V. The idea of leaving Hillsdale and resettling the whole family high in the Rockies paralleled George's own dream, fictionalized in his novel *Coming Home*. She, George, George V and Jake Roche could all have had a wonderful new life with Granaw at their side. Maybe IV would have realized the error of his ways and joined them.

Eager to understand her enthusiasm, I made my own winter visit to the region of Colorado that the Roche family considered a kind of spiritual home. Arriving at the tail end of a blizzard, it was easy to see why Lissa Roche hoped for a new beginning here. The region she had in mind is distinguished by four promontories honoring campuses far removed from the wild west, Mount Princeton, Mount Yale, Mount Columbia and Mount Harvard. Adding a new dimension to the meaning of higher education, each of these 14,000-foot-high peaks was scaled by an Ivy League climbing club with naming rights going to the first school team to reach the summit.

While visitors draw inspiration from these peaks rimming the Arkansas Valley, another landmark located a few miles to the south is the region's spiritual home. Here Mt. Shavano is a memorial to an Uncompaghre Ute war chief who patrolled this domain as white settlers wrested control of the mountain region from native Americans. Second in command to Chief Ouray, he was based on the state's western slope but made several lengthy trips a year to the Ute's Arkansas Valley domain.

Today this region's principal communities, Buena Vista and Salida, boast a mixed economy built around ranching, tourism, rafting and the prison business. But in Shavano's day the white man was still an outsider. As one of Shavano's biographers, Una Hogue, explained, "He was as true an Indian as ever lived. He was greatly opposed to giving up this country to the white man."[107] Honest and fearless, Shavano's real name was Tarbookchaket but he went by a name chosen by fur traders, Chaveneaux, which means blue flower or wild larkspur. In time, officials at the Los Pinos Indian Agency transliterated this to Shavano.

Shavano's three marriages were a disaster. In fits of anger, he shot one wife and went on to murder another, a beautiful young woman named Ceborow. Unpunished for this homicide, Shavano built a good reputation with many of the early white settlers who came to visit the Ute lands. He dined with the visitors and even lived with settlers for a short time when a blizzard made travel impossible. After a white child was badly injured it was Shavano who kept a vigil and prayed at his bedside. After the funeral Shavano and six other tribal members made a final tribute by riding past the grave with their arms raised high.

Shavano

The war chief could also be a tough negotiator. In 1868, a government agent refused to deliver Indian supplies for three months. When the war chief showed up with three thousand Indians to inquire about the holdup, the agent declined to hand out the supplies. Shavano and his Ute warriors reached under their blankets, brought out rifles and trained them on the agent's head. The supplies were distributed immediately. After Chief Ouray's death, Shavano was expected to succeed him. But federal officials, frightened of the war chief, rigged the election and threw it to another Native American leader.

Remaining a powerful force in the tribe, Shavano saw the continued white invasion of the former Ute homelands as an apocalypse. His concern was heightened by a series of gold and silver strikes in Chalk Creek Gulch midway between Salida and Buena Vista that transformed the region's economy. By the early 1880s over 50 miners were working the Gulch and rail service had been extended from the Arkansas Valley up Chalk Creek to St. Elmo.[108]

Shavano continued to protect his tribe as best he could and also began serving as a Ute medicine man. In 1885 he was called to attend to two boys shortly before they died. Rumors circulated that they had been poisoned by Shavano. A few days later while the war lord was standing in front of a trading post complaining to tribal members about white invaders shrinking the reservation lands, one of the boys' fathers walked up and fatally shot the war chief.[109]

After Shavano's death the people of Chaffee County decided to name a local peak in his honor. At the local library, I learned that this mountain inspired a legend immortalized in a Heart of the Rockies Chamber of Commerce brochure. The story, taught to every school child in the region, begins with a mischievous goddess who irked Jupiter by her pranks. In a fit of temper, Jupiter flash froze her into an icy white angel.

"Until some mishap or tragedy of other people moves you to tears, you will remain on Mount Shavano."

Left homeless on Mt. Shavano, the Angel lived for an eternity on the jagged mountain looking down upon her prosperous people who farmed industriously in the fertile valley. Happy and contented she saw the region transformed. The Indians were vanquished, then the bison disappeared. Finally new settlers arrived who did not roam the land like the Indians or dance around the camp fire. Happy and content, the angel had no complaints about her treatment at the hands of Jupiter.

But then a drought descended on the valley, the river dried up, the crops died and the angel tried to find a way to help her people pull out of this crisis. Depressed and plagued by a hopeless feeling, she began to cry and her tears melted her icy limbs. The angel literally began to thaw and her icy body began to crash down the mountain. Her tears triggered a massive snowmelt that flowed down into the valley. Soon the rivers ran swift and the drought was over. The farmers could go back to work.

And now, as the Heart of the Rockies brochure explained to visitors, "The angel thought to herself, 'My eyes will soon be gone also and I can no longer see my people grow well and strong again.' Her eyes were straining to join the rest when she heard a voice say, 'Angel of Shavano, you served your people well. In cold months of the year you will stand there as before, but when the warm winds come you will send your icy body down to aid your people.'

"The angel took a long searching gaze at her people and her eyes melted and dropped down to the river. You will see the 'Angel of Shavano' in the Spring months poised majestic and beautiful on Mount Shavano, the 'angel of Shavano,' who loved her people so well that each summer she gives her life to them that they may survive."[110]

During my visit to Shavano's homeland, I spoke with friends of the Roche family. One of them was Dorothy Roman, a Buena Vista teacher who had attended night school with George Roche and thought highly of his family. She suggested that returning to Colorado was not the answer to the family's prayers. When the Roche family ascended Hillsdale's Piety Knob and moved into Broadlawn, they brought with them a respect for family and homeland, a belief system that set an example for young people and most of all, a conviction that the Freewill Baptist tradition could now enrich the secular community.

But Lissa's dream of descending that hill and going to the mountaintop in Colorado proved impossible. Judging the family from Christmas cards she received each December, Roman believed Roche family values had been compromised. "The emphasis was always on the elegance of their lifestyle. Each picture showed the family arranged in the mansion or in front of the mansion. The idea was to show how grand the family had become. It was a total reversal of his original standards and ideals. . . . It's kind of like all those people coming in from California, building their big houses and driving up taxes. To them perception is everything. The whole focus is on personal gratification. People here don't like it."

Back in Michigan, Lissa decided to continue working under changed circumstances. She edited *Imprimis* and books for the Hillsdale College Press at home while a colleague, Jon Corombos, took over the Center for Constructive Alternatives events along with the Shavano Institutes. These changes, something Roche conceded he should have done much earlier, were helpful. But colleagues such as John Cervini, the school's director of development, recognized that slowing down was probably not enough. Lissa's problem was quite possibly a broken heart.

"Lissa was always in the main nice to me and my family and a very talented writer. I never saw anyone who could write as well as her and she was an organized person and committed . . . (she had) a lot of work and I am sure it took its toll, working to 1 or 2 A.M. She met her deadlines. I knew she had some distress with her son. He had problems with school and she was distressed that he wasn't doing better in school. He is a nice boy and has everything going for him and she felt embarrassed that he wasn't picking it up, acting like a 20-year-old. She was pretty upset about it and it bothered her. . . . I think she was trying to be caretaker for the family, that was part of it, to be the head of the household, tutoring Jake. . . . I had this e-mail message (on September 8) and I read it, boy she must be stressed out. . . . To me you don't up and leave after many years (working for the college) without saying goodbye to some people. . . . I was surprised by what she said in the memorandum about the divorce. . . . It sounded like she was stressed out and left for a couple of days, and then I heard that she had come back, but I didn't see her. . . . I think she was terribly embarrassed that she had left and that she had said those things. . . . I think that there are things we know now that were not known before. People couldn't put two and two together. It was unfortunate."[111]

During the second week of October, Lissa flew to California with the Hillsdale team for a Shavano at the Westin Hotel in Costa Mesa. Although she was no longer managing these events, Lissa continued to enthusiastically respond to speeches by distinguished guests such as Steve Allen, University of California Regent Ward Connerly, *Hating Whitey* author David Horowitz, and syndicated journalist Cal Thomas. Also on hand were a number of good friends including Pia and Dan York who were attending their first Shavano. Although the Yorks found Thomas's remarks disappointing, Lissa was impressed and told the author he was a shoo-in for an upcoming issue of *Imprimis*.

Pia York noticed that Lissa seemed a bit subdued and George Roche speculated to friends that perhaps she was "on something" such as a sedative. Dean Hagan shared her concern, particularly after Lissa slapped her on the back and asked, "Are you really having a good time?"[112] Noticing Lissa's glazed-over look, she also wondered if Lissa might have been on prescription medication.[113]

On Friday, October 15, after flying home from California, Lissa received great news. Roche walked over to the stone cottage and asked his daughter-in-law to help prepare papers for an annulment. Apparently, Roche had bought Lissa's argument that marriage to Dean was a mistake. By returning to Broadlawn, she and IV could help rebuild the extended family. Her trump card was George's delicate health which, she argued, could not withstand the stress of a marriage to a woman who didn't understand what it took to be a Roche. Ecstatic, Lissa phoned IV, who was at the George Roche Health Education and Sports Complex, and asked him to rush home.

The following day Lissa celebrated her decisive victory by taking her son Jake and his good buddy Nicholas York fishing. In an upbeat moment, she obligingly posed for a snapshot by holding a trout to her lips and puckering up.[114]

Late Saturday evening, October 16, there was a setback and a crisis. Dean Hagan called the stone cottage. George was having a major insulin reaction. IV rushed over to Broadlawn and tried to help him with glucogen tablets. Shortly after IV left, Dean went to the bedroom with a glass of milk and discovered George was having difficulty breathing. She called an ambulance. At the emergency room, doctors found that his blood sugar level was dangerously low and also diagnosed a heart arrhythmia. After rushing down to the emergency room, IV returned home at 3 P.M. and told Lissa that George and Dean "have reconciled." Lissa drove to the emergency room where she found George with his bride at his bedside. She demanded that Dean leave.

"If you don't get out of here," she told his new wife, a registered nurse, "and let me take care of him, he will be dead in one week."

Dean replied, "Lissa, please leave. He's in a lot of trouble and we need to take care of him."[115]

Lissa replied angrily in a voice that rang out so loudly hospital staff asked her to leave.

The next morning, George received a call from Lissa in his hospital room.

"Can't we all go back to Buena Vista?" she asked.

George explained why this was impossible. His marriage, the complicated lives of other family members, job commitments—there was no way that the Roches could retreat to the homeland he had celebrated in his novel.

Lissa responded by threatening to take her life.[116] After she hung up, Roche called his secretary, Pat Loper.[117] At his request she jumped in her car and immediately tracked down IV in a field outside of Jonesville where he was teaching a shooting class. While he and Dean waited to hear from IV, George rested in his bed, waiting for the doctor to arrive and check the heart monitor for arrhythmias. Exhausted from the overnight ordeal, Dean Hagan glanced over at George and said, "For some reason I don't feel comfortable with my back to the door."

When Loper dropped IV off at Broadlawn, Lissa appeared fine to him. But when IV told his wife that he'd been informed of her suicide threat, she became upset and demanded that they return to the hospital. When the couple arrived at the medical center, Lissa, dressed in a white t-shirt and a pair of "Hillsdale College" shorts, was clearly upset. Hagan asked her to leave.

"Just give me 10 minutes, nursie," Lissa asked.

"You have 10 minutes," Hagan replied.[118]

Roche, IV and Hagan listened to an indictment that added a very personal dimension to Lissa's coarse wedding party comments. The man she had worshiped as friend, father-in-law and co-worker was described as "scum of the earth." For the past 19 years, Lissa announced, she and her father-in-law had been carrying on a secret love affair.

"I could have believed her up to that point," Hagan said afterward. "But when she went on to allege that George had engaged in numerous affairs with Hillsdale coeds there was no way I could have believed her.

"I think she felt that life with her own family was hopeless. She was divorcing IV and then she and George could be free. IV was free to remarry with no guilt and then she and George and the children could live elsewhere and see each other. I don't think that Lissa was that sexual of a person. I think what she wanted was a fantasy that she had when she first went to Hillsdale. Now it was finally in her reach. She was this other woman patiently waiting. She lost control when she was out in California and found out that George was getting married. I was the 'other woman' who appeared out of nowhere. She had all the behaviors of someone who did not get their way."[119]

After Lissa's 10 minutes were up, she and IV returned home to the stone cottage. IV went back to his father's hospital room a few minutes later. Sitting down on the nearby empty bed, he looked at his father and asked:

"Dad, I just want to know the truth. Is what Lissa said the truth?"

"No," George told him, "I have never touched your wife."[120]

Hagan accompanied IV out of the room. In the corridor IV said he was worried about his wife's threat to harm herself. He wanted to get her immediate help. Hagan told IV to get Lissa back to the hospital immediately where doctors could prescribe medication. "Whatever you do," Hagan told him, "don't let Lissa out of your sight."[121]

Before leaving the hospital he contacted a nurse and a physician about Lissa's suicide threat. He also called a friend who used to work for Lifeways, a suicide prevention organization, and she agreed to help Lissa.[122]

When he returned to the stone cottage, IV found Lissa had not abandoned her dream. "You need to go back and see your dad and tell him we all need to leave Hillsdale and go somewhere else and start over."[123]

A little earlier that morning Lissa had carried soup and a book to Granaw at Broadlawn. Now she asked IV to head over to the house and check in on his grandmother. There were many good reasons for IV not to comply. His father, his father's secretary and his stepmother, a registered nurse, had all warned IV about Lissa's threat to take her life. IV himself had just sought professional help for his despondent wife. He even had a phone number for emergency crisis support. With a quick call any friend of the family, including his mother, his sister or a neighbor would have happily looked in on Granaw. Lissa had a key to a locked gun case in the stone cottage. And she had just angrily announced a 19-year affair with his father. If anyone demanded his immediate attention it was Lissa, not Granaw.

Now we have a confusing account: The drive from the stone cottage to Broadlawn, eight doors away, takes about a minute. IV says he complied with Lissa's wishes, arriving at Broadlawn at approximately 12:30 P.M.[124] Hagan did, independently, confirm that she and George had returned to Broadlawn from the hospital at about 12:30 P.M.[125] IV claimed he did not enter the mansion because he ran into his father and Dean who had just returned home from the hospital. But Granaw, George, and Dean Hagan have all denied ever seeing him pull up to Broadlawn.

At 1:14 P.M. Lissa's husband picked up the phone and dialed 911. "Hello, this is George Roche. My wife just shot herself."[126]

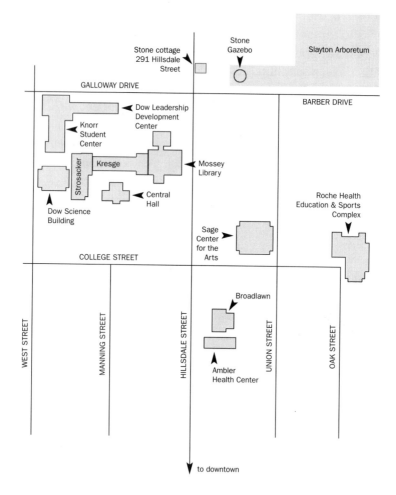

5

Hearing the Key Turn
in the Lock of Time

*"One could not go through Watergate and claim much
distinction for anything, but the fact was that I testi-
fied under oath 44 times and I was the only defen-
dant who was not charged with perjury. My dad's
lesson stuck: tell the truth."*
—Charles Colson, *Imprimis,* April 1993

WHEN HILLSDALE POLICE PATROLMAN Randy Casler
arrived at the corner of Hillsdale Street and Barber Drive, the 911 caller, cell phone in hand, climbed into the
back seat. He directed the officer to the first gate of the peace-
ful arboretum where nothing ever seemed to go wrong save
an occasional UFO sighting that turned out to be nothing
more than swamp gas. They found Lissa lying in a pool of
blood on the gazebo floor, clothed in the same t-shirt and
shorts she had worn to the hospital. Her jewelry included a
gold necklace with a St. Christopher medallion. Lissa's life
had ended with a single bullet to the right temple, apparently
fired from a stainless steel .357 magnum owned by her hus-

band. The heavy gun with a four-inch barrel and a gray pillow were found near her body.

"After examining the victim," patrolman Casler said, "I went back to Roche to interview him. At that time, I was not aware of who he was or his relationship to the victim. I was met by officer (Tom) Gaskell and advised him that we needed to get ahold of college security as I felt that this was a college student and that we needed to identify her. I turned to Roche and asked him how he hap-

The gazebo

pened to find the victim and he stated that the victim was his wife.... I asked Roche if he recognized the weapon and he stated that the gun was his and that it was kept in a cabinet. Roche then stated that he was concerned that his son would be arriving in the area as he lived at the Delta Tau Delta house and that he did not want him to see her. I advised him that I would take care of that."[127]

While police investigators converged on the death scene, one of George Roche's neighbors, Megan Angell, notified him of the tragedy. He headed down the street in running shoes and sweats. By the time he arrived, June Roche was already on the scene.

"For your personal happiness," she told her ex-husband, "you've taken our family as if we're a sheet of glass and broken it all over the sidewalk."[128]

After giving IV a chance to confirm with his father that his chosen funeral home performed cremations, the police asked IV to fill out a statement at the station house. Although he appeared calm, IV explained that he needed something to eat to relieve stomach troubles brought on by stressful situations. The police responded by offering to take him out for a quick lunch. On the way to the restaurant, IV mentioned to patrolman Gaskell that after 22 years of marriage, Lissa had changed dramatically during the past month. She had, according to IV become "flighty and depressed." Summarizing his conversation with IV, patrolman Gaskell would write, "Lissa was very depressed about George III's divorce and remarrying so quickly. Both Lissa and George IV were having a difficult time with their son, George, attending Hillsdale College. Lissa was also upset about George IV's 15-year-old brother, Jake, who was attending Hastings Public School and living with George IV's sister in Hastings. The brother's (actually his son George V's) academic performance at Hillsdale College had dropped since his parents' divorce and his father remarried. . . . George IV advised Lissa had left him for a couple of days earlier this month but she had moved back home and they were attempting to work out their problems."[129]

IV interrupted his story at Burger King where he ordered a Whopper Jr. with cheese and a Sprite.[130] This was just a short distance from the Big Boy where he and Lissa had first met in 1975.

At the police station, IV called his department head, explaining that he would not be able to teach additional classes the following semester. Then he broke the horrifying news of Lissa's death. Next he called another friend to congratulate him about an event and followed up with word of the suicide. After being asked for a written statement, IV said he wanted to speak with an attorney. Hillsdale College Provost Robert Blackstock, agreed to come down to the station house and meet with IV. After explaining that he had placed his law license in escrow, the administrator spoke with IV privately in the main hallway.[131] "I was there as a friend at that point," Blackstock said. "I did not know what he was upset about at that point."[132]

Following this conversation, IV failed to mention Lissa's account of a 19-year love affair with his father in a written statement for the police.[133] After completing his account, IV continued to phone friends, family and colleagues. Gaskell, who was with IV from 2:25 P.M. to 5:30 P.M. noted that "never once did George IV cry, even while making numerous phone calls from the station. George IV never showed outward signs of being emotionally upset over Lissa's death...."[134]

Reactions to tragedy are always a great unknown. IV has not made himself available to me or others to tell of his feelings about Lissa, his father or other events discussed in this book.

By the time the funeral home took possession of Lissa's remains, it was almost 5 P.M. Investigating officers headed for the stone cottage to begin a search of the premises. IV agreed to meet them after checking in on his grandmother at Broadlawn. On the ride home from the police station, IV finally told Hillsdale vice president Bob Blackstock about Lissa's allegations of a 19-year affair with the college president.[135]

After arriving at the stone cottage, IV agreed to reconstruct his actions leading up to the discovery of the body. In checking the arboretum area beyond the gated yard, officer Martin "noted a very narrow pathway which was covered with fallen pine needles. An area of pine needles near the gate seemed to be disturbed. However, in following the path down toward the gazebo and to a series of stone steps, the undersigned did not see any areas where the pine needles appeared to be disturbed. In the earlier interview with George IV, he stated that after finding the gate unlatched, he checked the path and steps which lead to the lower gazebo and observed areas in which the pine needles appeared to be disturbed. For that reason, he continued down the path toward the gazebo, looking for his wife. . . ."[136]

After finding her corpse and calling 911, IV explained to Martin "that his gun cabinet was locked and upon checking further, the pistol case was also locked. However, the gun was missing. Also, he noted that one of his speed loaders had been emptied. . . . George was asked how it was that Lissa gained access into the locked cabinet and retrieved the gun. He stated that both she and their son had keys to the gun cabinet which were kept on their key rings. When asked if Lissa was familiar with handguns, George replied that she had been shooting with him on prior occasions but he did not believe she had ever shot that particular gun."[137]

At this point, a routine police investigation should have encompassed the following:

• A fingerprint analysis of the .357, as well as the cabinet where the weapon had been stored and the keys used to open the cabinet. In addition, police needed to do a fingerprint test of the spent bullet, the unused bullets and the speedloader.

• A ballistics test of the .357. Here experts fire an identical bullet and match marks on the spent casing with the one retrieved from the arboretum. Specific milling characteristics of the gun would enable authorities to confirm that this gun was actually used to end Lissa's life.[138]

• Confirmation of the witness's statement that he was elsewhere when his wife died. This could have been accomplished by interviewing anyone who might have seen the witness around the time of Lissa's death.

• A search for the key ring holding the key Lissa would have used to unlock and relock the gun cabinet.

• Preparation and release of a complete autopsy report on Lissa's death.

• A gunpowder residue test on the dead woman and her husband.

• A search of the terrain adjacent to the incident for other material evidence.

For a variety of reasons the Hillsdale Police failed to accomplish any of these tasks or they performed them without success. In some cases, such as the autopsy, the authorities decided to suppress part of the document.[139] The ballistics test was never conducted. No fingerprints were found on the gun cabinet or the gun. Lissa was not wearing gloves, and, if she fired the bullet into her temple, she could not have wiped the gun clean. The keys used to unlock the cabinet are unaccounted for.[140] While samples were taken for a gunpowder residue test from both Lissa's and IV's hands, for no known reason these tests were never completed. In addition the police report makes it clear there was never a search of the general terrain in the vicinity of the incident.

There is also one other unusual fact about the police report. Officers I consulted have told me that the sound of a .357 being fired can be heard more than a mile away. How is it possible that this weapon fired in broad daylight in the popular arboretum, just a few hundred yards from a densely inhabited neighborhood, was heard by no one?

Perhaps the most interesting anomaly of all is a dispute between IV and his family over his whereabouts during the period just before Lissa's death. IV has stated that, at the time Lissa died, he was driving eight doors down Hillsdale Street to look in on his grandmother at Broadlawn. He told police that he canceled this errand when he arrived at the mansion and he met his father and Dean returning from the hospital.

Dean Hagan has told me that she, IV's father and Granaw never saw IV on this errand.[141] When I pointed this out to Hillsdale Police Detective Brad Martin, he told me his department never asked about this matter in their interviews with President Roche and Dean Hagan. In addition, Hagan told me she and Roche pulled up at the mansion around 12:30 P.M., the time IV originally told police he drove to Broadlawn. If IV was only gone for 5 minutes, this means he returned home approximately 40 minutes before finding Lissa in the arboretum and calling in her death. Requests for information on this puzzling matter and other subjects must be submitted to the police department in writing.[142]

While the detectives sifted through the evidence, IV took the story he earlier told Blackstock and withheld from the Hillsdale police to a larger audience. Not long after Lissa died, he explained to *National Review* reporter John J. Miller the story of Lissa's allegations of a 19-year affair with his father. "In the hours and days after the death," wrote Miller, "George IV—who had suffered blows that stagger and sicken the imagination—began to sense that the college was going to spin the suicide: He thought the college was going to say, 'Here was a woman who simply went crazy.' And that, he insists, 'is just a f***ing lie.'"[143]

IV's contention that the college was going to use Lissa's charges of an affair to destroy her reputation was difficult to comprehend. After all he was the one who broke the news of Lissa's charges, not to police investigators but to a top college official.

Another source of confusion was the medical examiner's

decision to only release part of the autopsy report because it contains information of a "personal nature."

"If the court wants to rule it, I'll go along with it," said Dr. Tom Noll, Hillsdale County Medical Examiner, when asked about the possibility of releasing the balance of the report. "For my own personal opinion, I regard it as more of a gossip center and detrimental to some of the people involved in the situation. My job is to safeguard other people from being hurt."[144]

Detective Martin agreed. "We're just trying to make appropriate decisions and offer protection for the family." He added that the department agreed with the medical examiner's request not to release the full autopsy.[145]

"In a case like this there was some suspicion among the public. Some didn't feel it was a suicide. Both the son and father corroborated each other's story that she was despondent. Then you have the medical examiner and the coroner both concluding it was a suicide. Since the police did not dust the gun cabinet for fingerprints or take possession of the keys she used to unlock and lock the cabinet, it is not possible to independently corroborate this part of the story. You are going to always have peculiarities in a case. You will have people who will ask why would you lock the gun cabinet.... Anyone in this investigation would want to keep an open mind."[146]

Since Detective Martin is no longer speaking to me and all my requests for information must now be submitted in writing, it seems unlikely that any new evidence will emerge from the Hillsdale Police Department. The plot they have outlined is so farfetched that I doubt a novelist or screenwriter would take it seriously. It sounds unlikely that someone would unlock and lock a gun case, shoot themselves and leave behind no keys. The lack of fingerprints or a gunpowder residue test add to the mystery. And why would a responsible police department skip a ballistics test of the weapon in question?

After Lissa's cremation, IV's sister Maggie made arrangements for the public visitation three days after Lissa's death. June greeted guests in the lobby area of the Van Horn-Eagle Funeral Home. Inside the funeral parlor's double doors were George and Dean Hagan. At the far end of the room were the rest of the Roche and Jackson families including IV, George V, Maggie, Muriel, Lissa's father and her sisters Linda and Laura. Jake circulated freely around the room. A number of the guests did a double take when they spotted Lissa's identical twin sister Laura, beautifully dressed in one of Lissa's best outfits. "I'm wearing Lissa's clothes," she confided to those who were used to seeing the editor in more mannish apparel. Lissa's ashes were on a table near the receiving line.

At the funeral, Professor Willson said, "We will never fully understand what caused her hope to diminish. But we should remember that the lines from Chesterton's poem that she loved so well are followed by this stanza:

The gods lie dead where the leaves lie red,
For the flame of the sun is flown.
The gods lie cold where the leaves lie gold,
And a Child comes forth alone."

Although it wasn't read at the service, another quote from her friend and Hillsdale lecturer Malcolm Muggeridge, one she published in her 1995 anthology, *A Christian's Treasury of Stories and Songs, Prayers and Poems, and Much More for Young and Old* would have also been appropriate:

"So, like a prisoner awaiting his release, like a schoolboy when the end of term is near, like a migrant bird ready to fly south, like a patient in the hospital anxiously scanning the doctor's face to see whether a discharge may be expected, I long to be gone, extricating myself from the flesh I have too long inhabited, hearing the key turn in the lock of Time."[147]

Rejoined for Lissa's funeral just barely a month after the Roche-Hagan wedding, the family was now on the edge of another tragedy, one that would deprive Lissa of the anonymity she sought when she resigned and left IV in September. For George Roche the issue was no longer merely the breakup of the extended family. Without Lissa, it was difficult to imagine continuing at Hillsdale. There was no way for him to rationalize the mistakes he had made such as loving Lissa in a way that breached the boundaries of common sense and letting her personal loyalty create a working relationship that was unhealthy for all concerned. Lissa's anger in the hospital room may have led her to stretch the truth. But even if they had not been lovers, there was no doubt that their passion for each other had helped destroy both of their marriages and careers. Was it conceivable that it would destroy Hillsdale College too?

Uncertain about whether or not to postpone his honeymoon in Hawaii, Roche consulted the trustees. When they encouraged him to go, perhaps hoping that his absence would quiet the campus, he and Dean headed to the Detroit airport. By the time the newlyweds landed in Hawaii, IV had visited with Blackstock, the same man he had called for assistance at the police station following his wife's death. Although Blackstock already knew about Lissa's allegations of an affair, IV was now addressing him in an official capacity. Again, IV focused on Lissa's side of the story. But he did not mention her allegations of George Roche's affairs with coeds. (I for one find this astonishing.) If he believed his wife had slept with his father, why would he not believe her accusation that he also slept with students? If true, this second allegation threatened to irrevocably damage the future of Hillsdale College.

I believe that IV did not repeat charges that his father slept with students because he guessed that they were not credible. That implies Lissa, at the end of her life, was not a fully credible witness to the behavior of George Roche. By extension it would be logical to conclude that IV has created at best, an incomplete picture of her final hours. Considering the fact that Lissa had told the entire campus she was divorcing her husband and that she suspected he was having an affair, it's hard to be sure of his motivation, especially when he married the woman in question a few months after his wife's death.

IV insisted his father had refused to answer his direct question about the truth of Lissa's accusations. The president insists that he did answer this question negatively. IV's selective approach, which he had also taken at the police department, was completely understandable to Provost Blackstock. As the administrator explained, "He had no intention of not telling them why she was upset. The poor guy had just found his wife dead by her own hand, and he was crushed."[148]

Blackstock took up the matter with vice-president Trowbridge, who contacted the board of trustees. They responded by calling an emergency meeting of the college's prudential committee. Twelve hours after arriving in Hawaii, George and Dean Roche called off their honeymoon and headed home. By the time they touched down in Michigan, the couple had survived the airline industry's equivalent of a near-death experience. They had been forced to watch, on four separate planes in two days, what many critics agreed was one of the worst movies of the decade, *Wild Wild West,* starring Will Smith and Salma Hayek.

On November 1 the trustees placed George Roche on a leave of absence. Provost Blackstock, the first person IV told about Lissa's alleged affair with George Roche, was named acting president of Hillsdale College.

6

He Can Run, But He Can't Hide

RETURNING FROM HAWAII, George Roche and Dean Hagan were in exile shortly after their jet touched down. The Detroit area would become their temporary Elba. With Central Hall on red alert over IV's sensational charges of adultery, the first couple was asked not to return to Hillsdale until the board of trustees had an opportunity to review the matter. The possibility of putting the newlyweds up at the Munro House, a circa 1830 bed and breakfast that had once been a hiding place for blacks on the Underground Railroad, was rejected for security reasons. Located just five miles from Hillsdale, it was considered too close to IV, who was now rumored to be carrying a gun in self-defense.[149] IV had become the point man in a drama that threatened not only his father but the reputation of the entire campus. Were he to divulge the entire scope of Lissa's charges against her father-in-law, including sex between the president and coeds, the school would be seriously damaged.

Roche once said that "you cannot do what I've done for so long without having people who are upset." For most of his career the complainers were employees, students, some alumni and an occasional holier than thou writer compelled to stage a journalistic *jihad* against the college. But pitted against the board of trustees and denied access to his own office, he was unable to make a special pleading. As president, Roche had always insisted on three guiding principles to any controversy: "Seize the issue, seize the moment to present the issue, give your own definition to the debate."

Now there was no one to take the helm. Roche blamed himself for doing a poor job of preparing a presidential succession plan. Without a strong leader on the scene Hillsdale College was unable to beat back the critics eager to second-guess the handling of Lissa's death. At a meeting of the full board on November 10, Roche read aloud a three-page single-spaced letter he had written to IV, with copies to his children Maggie, Muriel and Jake. He asked the board to suspend disbelief and hear the survivor's side of the extraordinary relationship that had begun shortly after Lissa's marriage to IV.

There was, he conceded, great love between himself and Lissa. Denying this passion had been the greatest mistake of his life. For 20 years, he managed to hide the truth from the rest of his family and the college community at large. While he denied that he had been sexually involved with Lissa, he freely conceded that they enjoyed a remarkable intimacy. Lissa's sister Laura, the president proudly pointed out, said that she and Lissa had openly discussed how much Lissa and he had loved one another. Voicing guilt over his failure to do more for Lissa in the final hours of her life, Roche told the board that he loved Lissa with all his heart and always would. There was no doubt in his mind that she loved him as well.

He explained how Lissa had served as a surrogate mother to his children in the midst of a frequently unhappy and dysfunctional marriage. She loved and cared for the entire fam-

ily. Lissa was a co-worker, close family member, dear friend
and best buddy. There was a strong emotional attachment but,
he insisted adultery was never a part of their friendship. Lissa's
marriage was increasingly troubled and the couple had
recently discussed the possibility of divorce. George V was
doing badly in school and reached the point in his life where
his mother's strong guidance had become most unwelcome.
There had been a number of acrimonious confrontations between Lissa and her son. Convinced that she had lost George
V, Lissa was particularly angry at IV for what she saw as a
lack of support in her efforts to save their son from flunking
out of college.

This situation was complicated, as the board well knew, by
Lissa's unacceptably heavy workload. Perhaps, he suggested,
she had given too much to her loved ones and did not have
enough energy left to sustain herself. When IV and Lissa
moved into Broadlawn and established an extended family
her life became even more complicated. Family and campus
obligations pushed Lissa to the point where Roche belatedly
decided to reassign the Center for Constructive Alternatives,
Von Mises lectures and Shavano programs to others. Roche
believed that making that decision earlier might have saved
Lissa's life.

When Roche conceded to the trustees that this mistake
was one that he would regret to his dying day, the board members began to realize that the letter was an excruciating confession. As a number of them knew, Roche had, after his divorce
from June, been eager to remarry. What they did not know was
that his September 13 wedding to Hagan was strongly opposed
by Lissa. Although she had attended the wedding with IV,
there was no doubt in her mind that this decision would destroy
the extended Broadlawn family she had built from the wreck-

Broadlawn

age of his first marriage. As Roche explained it, they had been a team, professionally and personally, caring for the college, for Granaw and young Jake. His mother, his children, IV and V and her father-in-law were the world to her. Hurt and angry over her apparent rejection by George III, IV and George V, and battling with June over Jake's schoolwork, she was reduced to a caretaker role for Granaw.

Instead of responding to her anger and erratic behavior, Roche continued on a course that appeared to add to her confusion, first asking her to work on an annulment and then reversing himself. His explanation of the hospital room showdown stunned the board. They listened as he explained how Lissa burst into the emergency room at 3 A.M., demanding that Dean leave so that the family could have privacy.

At 10 A.M., after he had moved into a hospital room with Dean, Lissa was back, demanding, once again, that she be given an audience. It was here that the woman who had been the president's most loyal aide and collaborator, staunchest defender and leading ally broke down. She characterized her father-in-law as a terrible person who had been having an affair with her for the past two decades. She continued to allege numerous affairs with others. When Dean refused to discuss these allegations until Lissa calmed down, she remained distraught and left. IV followed her out of the room and returned a few minutes later to confront his father who denied the allegations.

In a moment of great candor, he read the board the portion of his letter to his son, voicing his belief that IV and Lissa always had a normal sexual relationship. In the 25 years he had known Lissa, he had never seen sexually aggressive or promiscuous behavior. In all the years of this alleged affair, IV never confronted his father about this matter, Roche said. During the 10 days following Lissa's death the two men saw each other frequently. Again, during this time the subject of the affair never came up. Assigning sordid sexual overtones to Lissa's memory because of her anguish and distress at the end of her life soiled the memory of a wonderful woman who had spent much of her life loving and caring for the entire family, he said in the letter. Pass judgment if you must, he told IV, but don't carry a false and harmful picture of Lissa in your heart.

Looking down at the letter to his son, Roche tried to elevate the crisis to a higher level. Reminding IV that all of us will appear before our Ultimate Judge one day soon, Roche prayed for mercy on Lissa and the rest of the family for all the sins they had committed. Very possibly, the family will need God's mercy for the things they might have done and failed to do.

After asking for the forgiveness of Jesus he told IV that public knowledge of his alleged adulterous relationship with Lissa effectively ended his career at Hillsdale. He was retiring from the college and leaving as soon as final arrangements could be made. Expressing regret that his life's work concluded so badly, he voiced his love for IV. Uncertain of what lay ahead for the rest of his family he spoke of his love and concern for Jake, Granaw, Maggie, Muriel and George V, all victims in something none of them created.

"Right now," he concluded, "I do not know what lies ahead except that I am leaving Hillsdale. I do know that I love my family. All else is in God's hands."

The board's reaction to this astonishing letter was silence. There were no comments or questions, just a general feeling of relief that Roche was gone. Hurt that none of his trustee friends had spoken up for his side of the story, he left Central Hall and climbed into his car with Dean for an 1,100 mile drive to Colorado. The long trip took a mere 14 hours. Later he offered to publish a modified version of his remarks in *Imprimis*. It was, he suggested, the logical way to say goodbye to thousands of loyal supporters. His colleagues at Central Hall turned him down. Instead the trustees issued a brief statement, accepting Roche's resignation, thanking him for his fine work, voicing sorrow over Lissa's death and announcing formation of a search committee for a new president, with William F. Buckley as co-chair.

Initially, the couple considered relocating to northern Michigan. But as he traveled north to the Gaylord area, where the family had vacationed for many years, there was an inescapable feeling that people in stores, gas stations and restaurants were staring at him. It was almost as if someone had painted a crimson "A" down his back. Back home in Hillsdale his old colleagues heard rumors that gas station attendants had asked the former president if he was the man who had been sleeping with his daughter-in-law for two decades.

Roche and his wife decided that it would make more sense to relocate back in Colorado. They chose the Ouray area named for the leader of the Indian nation that had once ruled this mountain region. The couple moved to a home at the 9,000-foot level, began making renovations and welcomed back 91-year-old Granaw.

Unlike Aspen and Telluride, Ouray was a town that had managed to avoid becoming a real estate play for schuss-boomers. But the nearby mountain country had attracted many celebrities including designer Ralph Lauren, actor Dennis Weaver and a recent Shavano series headliner, General Norman Schwarzkopf. Roche hoped to make Ouray his Mt. Olympus, but the media gods were not in his favor. Within a short time it became his Götterdämmerung.

While moving in to his new home, the former president bid farewell to Hillsdale and those who had shared his vision with a brief letter he mailed to friends:

"Knowing that the passing years brought ever closer the time of my departure from Hillsdale, I had always wondered how to say goodbye. Now the time has come.

"In the grief and confusion surrounding the tragedy of Lissa's death, statements have been made that tarnish her memory. I must address those statements before I say goodbye. The details of my family's life should not be publicly discussed. Let it suffice to say that Lissa was a dear daughter to me for the last quarter century.... We shared an immense emotional attachment. I would gladly do anything to bring her back to us, but, before God, I deny any improper relationship....

"I say this for her memory, not for mine. Once such allegations are loose in the world, they take on a life of their own, no matter how false. Many of my friends know and believe the truth. To them I give my love and deep appreciation. For those who relish the details of an imaginary scandal which so unjustly injures my family and Lissa's memory, I ask God's mercy.

"In any case, it is time to leave Hillsdale. I am nearly 65 years old and no longer have a wish to continue. As I leave, I want to thank my many, many friends and co-workers. Together we built a wonderful school, a wonderful dream, We showed the way. We proved it could be done. Now that task is still in your hands. Hold the torch high. Show the world what courage, integrity and values can still mean, even in a badly corrupted world.

"For my part, I shall always remember the friends and the work with deep pride. I will also remember the good times and the wonderful friends of Hillsdale. You will always be in my thoughts and prayers."

One Hillsdale professor who did not receive Roche's letter was Dr. Michael Bauman, head of the Department of Christian Studies. When we met at my Jonesville bed and breakfast, the Munro House, he told me that he had already lost two of his most important students to the crisis. A former Evangelical Free Church minister, he characterized his job as showing students why "theology is within shouting distance of other disciplines. What difference does Christ mean to English and other disciplines. What should we be making of the Old Testament. If we can't get the word right, we can't get the world right.

"A novelist makes the world with words. How does Hemingway stack up to his obligation to make a world with words."

Now students were applying this test to a lesser-known

writer, George Roche. The two students who decided to quit did so because they did not want the Hillsdale leader's name on their degree. "I spoke to both those fellows and they decided the reasons for staying did not outweigh the reasons for leaving." One of them told Dr. Bauman, "I'm paying this university dollars to get this degree and now it would have this smudge on it."[150]

Like many people on campus, Bauman was dismayed by the board of trustees' refusal to confirm or deny IV's allegations, as reported in conservative journals like the *National Review* and the *Weekly Standard* and repeated by just about every newspaper and wire service in the land. One of the most significant parts of the story was IV's account of the moment when he confronted his father-in-law in the hospital with Lissa's charges of a sordid affair. In the *National Review* article, widely quoted by journalists, IV claimed that his father did not reply to his direct question. "I saw the look in his eyes. He was caught." Reporters trying to walk in to Broadlawn were tossed out by Dean. Young Jake Roche, away at high school in his sister Maggie's hometown of Hastings, needed a private escort home to slip past journalists stalking him in the school halls. Even the college's champions, such as Secretary of Education William Bennett, questioned the trustees' lack of openness. Were Lissa's charges true? If so, how long has this been going on? As he resigned from the school's new presidential search committee, Bennett told the media in mid-November 1999:

"A week ago, I was told it looked like the allegations were true. The first answer to my question was exactly, 'Sure, it is (true).' Then this week, I got, 'Well, we're not sure.' Then it was 60–40. And now it's a lot of talk about Lissa being a pathological liar. And this is where I got off."

Bennett, who had written a book criticizing the way the Clinton administration had tried to spin the Monica Lewinsky sex scandal, saw no reason to give George Roche the benefit of the doubt. "This institution is the shadow of this man and the 30 years of accomplishments he's made. But if this man fell short of his ideals and the ideals he was trying to impart we need to know that so we can say, 'This was a terrible thing,' and then move on. You can't move on until you tell the story. There's a dead woman here! There's a dead woman here. No it is not over. Not until they tell us the truth."[151]

Bennett's excellent statement was greeted with silence. No one else in a position of responsibility demonstrated his kind of courage. When he spoke out about Bill Clinton's excesses, the nation listened. When he asked the same kinds of questions about Lissa Roche, leaders ducked for cover. At the police department, details of the official investigation into Lissa's death were suppressed. At Central Hall, no one wanted to produce a meaningful statement on the validity of IV's spectacular allegations. None of the principals appeared willing to step forward and address Bennett's legitimate concerns. In a formal statement on November 22, 1999, provost Robert Blackstock acknowledged the school's critics:

"Recent discussions with students, faculty and staff regarding Dr. Roche's leave of absence and subsequent retirement suggest a certain lack of clarity. . . . First and foremost, events of recent weeks represent a terrible tragedy for the entire community, and most especially for the Roche family. As we all continue to recover from this loss, I would encourage everyone to continue reaching out to friends and colleagues, and to keep the Roche family in your prayers.

"The college has been faulted for not being more forthcoming with information, especially about the allegations of an affair. From the time Dr. Roche was placed on leave of absence on November 1, until approximately November 16, we were advised by counsel that details relating to the leave of absence and retirement were confidential and protected by a legal right of privacy. During this period we could not so much as confirm that allegations had been made. By November 16, however, counsel advised us that matters made public by the press were no longer private and could be addressed by the College. This memo and a series of meetings with College students, faculty, and staff are the result of these relaxed legal constraints.

"Allegations of an affair between Lissa Roche and Dr. Roche were made by Lissa just hours before she took her life. To this day, the Board does not know if the allegations are true or not. Dr. Roche denies the allegations. Given the paucity of evidence, we may never know if the allegations are true, but we are taking preliminary steps to make certain we are doing all that can and should be done.

"Of one thing though, the Board was confident. The swirl of rumors had so diminished Dr. Roche's credibility and authority that he could no longer govern. The Board's decision was driven by the conclusion that Dr. Roche simply could not continue to lead the College effectively.

"As we enter this holiday season, I pray that the pain of these difficult weeks may be soothed and wounds healed. And in this week of Thanksgiving, I pray that we might all remain grateful for those countless and inestimable blessings that have been given us by our Creator. May God bless."[152]

The college's inept statements infuriated Hillsdale loyalists like Bennett. And the media firestorm, particularly from conservative publications like the *National Review,* edited by their close friend William F. Buckley, was hard on the extended

Roche family. Like Lissa, June Roche had been a critical factor in Roche's success. Without her help and that of her daughter-in-law, it is not at all certain that Roche could have raised more money than George W. Bush and Al Gore combined, that he could have become a $300 million man. Yet even now, after her divorce, the death of her daughter-in-law, after her lashing out at Roche in front of Lissa and IV's house, she defended her former husband.

"This is a tragedy, a terrible thing, a terrible waste," said June. "I grieved for Lissa, I loved her." But when she heard people who had been having affairs of their own condemn Roche, she was hurt and angry about their hypocrisy and "lack of compassion. Someone wrote a 24-page article calling him a Catholic! . . . I'm just devastated by what happened and the way the conservative movement has turned on him. . . . It's like Richard Nixon. He had a tremendous foreign policy before Watergate and then that one thing blew everything apart. You do something important and and all of a sudden a monkey wrench is thrown in and it blows everything apart. . . . We don't know all the external factors that have contributed to this.

". . . God works in mysterious ways. This may have been God's chance to save George's soul and get him to a monastery. I said to George, 'I think what you built will survive. I don't think you'll get a retirement party. If you know what you believe is true you have to get yourself right with God."

Unraveling the chain of events that led to Lissa's death was complicated by the difference of opinion between her son and her former husband. "You have IV saying there was an affair and George saying it wasn't true."

June, who spent a fair amount of time helping her son sort through Lissa's belongings following her death, rejected the assumption floating around campus that novelist Ayn Rand's objectivist belief system helped explain Lissa's fascination with George. The idea that Roche was, in Lissa's mind, a latter-day John Galt, the hero of Rand's novel *Atlas Shrugged,* was ridiculous. Any serious interest Lissa had in Rand had certainly been left behind on the Flint School yacht. "There wasn't a single Ayn Rand novel on her bookshelf," June explained.

She believed her daughter-in-law's fascination with Roche had more in common with *Clifford, the Big Red Dog* than Rand's fiction. "A little girl hopes the dog becomes her protector. She didn't want him married (to Dean). As soon as he married this other woman she lost control. She wanted to control everything."[153]

Were Lissa and her father-in-law sleeping together? Some close friends of the family doubted this was the case. "I don't believe the worst about George," said author, commentator and frequent Hillsdale speaker Michael Medved. After mentioning that "this was not the first time Lissa and IV had separated," he said, "George and Lissa have been guests in my home on more than one occasion. I do believe that Lissa had a case of hero worship and a fixation on George. All of that creates a horrible situation. Lissa was a wonderful and talented person. The worst you can say about George is that he showed bad judgment in allowing Lissa to be so close to him for all those years. It is one of those things where people say you don't want your wife working with you because you can't fire her.

"You knew she was having a difficult time in her marriage and she was having a difficult time in her job. It's a small college. I've been on campus many times. Somebody would have suspected something. There are people like Ron Trowbridge (who might have known). It's not an easy thing to keep a secret. There was no one involved with Hillsdale who said 'Now the truth is out.'... Certain people, you say, 'this person is having an affair. This person is flirtatious. It's not surprising.' Lissa was not flirtatious. I think what happened (was) as long as June and George were married, Lissa was perfectly content ... everything was fine because George was unattainable."

Medved thinks that after the divorce "Lissa was thrilled to be acting as the president's wife at social events...."

"My very strong impression is that George's big mistake was allowing, even facilitating this. George like everyone else loves being a hero to people and to some extent he benefited a great deal with Lissa.

"She liked being the queen of the college. There was something a little bit disquieting about this. One time when I was there for the Center for Constructive Alternatives, she set up this breakfast in the president's room at the Dow Center for me, her and George. George wanted to speak to me about a couple of things. It was her pride in him."154

Unlike Medved, the police appeared to accept IV's story of his wife's relationship with his father, even if the investigators had to find out about it in the *National Review* and the newspapers. The fact that IV left out Lissa's allegations of Dr. Roche bedding down campus coeds raised an important question. Corroborating this information could help the police shed new light on the college president. The fact that none of Dr. Roche's alleged girlfriends have come forward to present evidence indicates that at least one part of Lissa's story remains unsubstantiated.

The significance of these allegations was certainly not lost on the family or trustees. In her last hours, Lissa dropped a bombshell that threatened Roche and Hillsdale College. If her charges were true, their significance went far beyond

Broadlawn. Who exactly were the coeds that had slept with the president? Might one or more of them come forward and plunge a former Freewill Baptist College into a tawdry sex scandal? Or was Lissa simply making all this up—about herself and other women in the manner of a disgruntled employee using smear tactics to damage her boss? By failing to fully investigate the matter, the trustees could end up in the embarrassing and dangerous position of contributing to a cover-up. Or perhaps they knew some things and just weren't telling? Likewise, other nagging questions abound in the Hillsdale community. Questions about the final hours of Lissa's life could be answered if the Hillsdale Police Department released the full autopsy report and IV made himself available to answer critical questions.

Does he have a suicide note that no one else has seen? Does he know someone else who saw Lissa pull the trigger? Did Lissa say something to him that has yet to be made public?

The police report makes it clear that IV omitted crucial details of Lissa's final hours in his initial statement to the authorities. He did not tell the police that Lissa had claimed she had a 19-year affair with her father-in-law. When he broke this story to the national media was he trying to shift the focus of attention away from a debate on the manner of Lissa's death? And why did he leave out charges that his father had slept with coeds?

Why have the police failed to release portions of the autopsy? They have not accounted for crucial pieces of evidence including fingerprints and gunpowder residue. No one in a position of responsibility in the Hillsdale Police Department feels a need to reopen the case. As William Bennett has pointed out, a woman is dead here and we still don't know the truth. And as Socrates told Glaucon, the ring of invisibility is always a limited time offer. Sooner or later the truth slips out. Or as a real heavyweight, Joe Louis, put it before stepping into the ring with Billy Conn: "He can run, but he can't hide."

7

Must Everybody Get Stoned?

*"We've always known, haven't we, that human beings
are fallen or depraved. Jeremiah was saying this long
ago. You can find objective confirmation of that every
day and recently we found it on campus."*
—Michael Bauman

As the police sidestepped the Roche case and the trustees searched for new leadership, the Hillsdale crisis was enough to inspire editorials and sermons from Phoenix to Boston. While the media focused on the Roche family, Bauman believed it was also important to look at the role played by the board of trustees: "If the allegations are false," Bauman said, "then the board has allowed an innocent man to be drummed out on the basis of false allegations.... If this is true someone must have known about it and those people are still in power.

"No one ever said to me in the years I've been here that Lissa was suicidal or delusional. Suicide is rare and a woman's suicide with a gun is extremely rare. IV is not the kind of man who would make it (the charges of a 19-year affair with George

Roche) up. Who would make it up when you are a poster boy for family values? Occasionally Lissa joked about marrying the wrong George.... It never occurred to me that it was more than a joke."

Adultery, Bauman reminded me, is a capital offense, a violation of the laws of Moses, in the Old Testament. But Christ believed that it was important to judge not only the accused, but the accuser. This gives us all a chance to redeem ourselves and go on to live an admirable life.

"'Should we stone her?' Jesus is asked by men who have brought him a woman caught committing adultery. If he says, 'Stone her,' he looks unforgiving and cruel. If he says 'Let her go,' he'll look licentious, like a libertine. He says, in one of the most famous lines in the Bible, 'Let him that is without sin cast the first stone.' He knew that they were trying to catch him. They weren't concerned about the woman. In one sentence he exposes the hypocrisy and deceit in her accusers.

"Then he says to the woman, 'Who condemns you?'"

"She says, 'No one.'"

"He says, 'Neither do I, go and sin no more.' He keeps the law and extends the forgiveness required for repentance.

"We've always known, haven't we, that human beings are fallen or depraved. Jeremiah was saying this. You can find objective confirmation of that every day and recently we found it on campus."

In this instance, Bauman told me, "The roles are all turned around. IV is in the position of the accuser, George is in the position of the woman and the board is in the position of Christ. Their decision doesn't deal with either man's shortcomings. Jesus's decision dealt with the spiritual shortcomings of the accused and the accuser." Here "neither one truly got addressed and it's obvious that both of these guys can't be right. The board in the end said, 'we can't tell, we don't know.' But to play it safe, they let George resign, they gave him his (retirement) money (rumored to be $2 million) and moved on. That is exactly what they did. I'm not comfortable with it because it leaves all the important questions unanswered. It is not that the board did wrong. It's that they were left in the position of not doing anything. We either have a false accuser or a guilty man.

"I'm not omniscient, I don't know the truth. Christ would know, God knows. . . . George III knows what the facts are. So does O.J. The frustration is aimed at the fact that the real truth won't come out with any clarity or finality. The fact that the two parties are both so close makes it even more frustrating.

"Who benefited from this? Nobody that I can see. I suppose I can see how George would benefit from saying from what he said, but I can't see how IV would benefit from what he said. In the end neither one of them benefited. They destroyed things for many people."[155]

In much the same way that Lenin statuary began disappearing after the fall of Communism, Lissa's death brought an end to Roche iconography at Hillsdale. A photograph of the school's former president was taken down from the fieldhouse. His name was dropped from campus publications. And for the first time he was no longer a Shavano headliner.

The adverse publicity began to have a negative impact on admissions applications. All this was highlighted on the Hillsdale Liberation Organization website featuring a chat room where students discussed the rise and fall of George Roche. Offering access to news and feature coverage of the crisis, the HLO also reported on subjects such as a lawsuit filed against the college by Mark Nehls, a student dismissed from the school after he began publishing an underground campus paper. "I like to compare the site to a vampire," said vice president Trowbridge. "It has to hide and work at night."

While the 10 percent drop in student applications was hardly a threat to Hillsdale's future, it did mirror the concerns of high school teachers who had touted the liberating influence of this conservative liberal arts college. Not long after Roche departed, Reist received a phone call from a high school instructor mortified by the scandal. "Professor," she asked, "I've been telling my students to go to Hillsdale College. What can I tell them now, I feel like I've been raped."

"We've all been raped," replied Reist.[156]

In a radio commentary, Hillsdale speaker and *Imprimis* contributor Charles Colson, who had been with Nixon during Watergate, suggested that the college had booby trapped itself with secularization. Yes, Roche had raised more money than any American presidential candidate. But this required severing the school's church ties, a serious mistake.

"What Roche was trying to do at Hillsdale ... was to create a strong pro-family, pro-traditional values institution—but keep it secular. Many politicians try to do the same thing, giving us the impression that we can create a good and just society on our own, without reference to a transcendent moral authority. It just doesn't work."

Contradictions were also on the mind of Reist who pastors Somerset Congregational Church, about 20 minutes from Hillsdale. Following services one Sunday afternoon, he said, "You have a man talking about family values, Christian faith and the importance of Hillsdale Academy and Christianity. They send their kids here because they have wearied of multiculturalism and political correctness. They want their kids to be addressed by the truth in the time-honored tradition.

"At Hillsdale students learn that democracy is necessary

because men are evil and they know it. Why do we have a balance of power between the three branches of government? Because we are sinners.

"If the board of trustees had been a little more prescient and not given George Roche carte blanche we wouldn't be where we are today. After saying the good things he did for the school, George Roche was not a man open to free debate in the tradition of classical liberation. His problem was spelled out long ago when Socrates said that the truth is hard to know because most people mistake their opinion for the truth.

"George Roche hasn't confessed for two reasons. His legal counsel told him not to and he doesn't think he has done anything wrong. There is no redemption without acknowledgment and confession. Redemption is not easy and it's not cheap. Redemption is not overlooking the truth. And you'll pardon me but what kind of grace of Christ is it without forgiveness and confession?"[157]

During our long conversation, Reist told me a story about Roche's legendary temper. Referring to Poliakoff, the classics professor who had discovered the infamous Grieb collection of anti-Semitic literature, Roche told Reist, "He's the best excuse I can think of for a pogrom."[158]

I asked Dr. Poliakoff, now working at an educational foundation in Washington, D.C., if he believed Reist's version of the conversation. "Some of my ancestors were killed in pogroms. I still find that comment so horrifying that I have trouble believing it, although I say the source that told me is someone whose integrity I have complete trust in.

"When you write this up, I want you to mention that in the ethnography of higher education quite a few college presidents have been fired because of the disease that comes from an autocratic leader. George Roche was certainly not alone.

There was the president of one east coast school making obscene phone calls and losing his job. It was a terrible scandal. These very vile obscene phone calls were traced back to the president's office and he claimed he was abused as a child. But the buck stops when these calls are traced back to the president's office. Similarly the president of another eastern college was fired for financial misdoings.

"You know there is wonderful devotion to principle and excellent education at Hillsdale. I watched the classics department grow to the size that would be the envy of a school three times it size. I love the academic world and might at some point go back. But this environment was turning very sour and I had to leave. The mischievousness was not the problem of a conservative institution. It's the problem of an autocrat.

"George Roche believed he was above reproach for so long that it made him incapable of believing that any action would be reproachful or reprehensible.... George got it wrong. You throw the ring of power into the fire. You destroy it for the same reason that the little hobbits destroy the power of Sauron. That is what they had to do in order to protect everything that they valued in the world. Holding on to this ring of autocracy is not the way that you forge a society, a community, and a college is a community. The ring of power corrupted him."[159]

Socrates' student Glaucon argued that people were honest because they were afraid of getting caught. But Socrates suggested that the mere fact Glaucon was making such an argument presaged the great moment when philosophers became kings and kings became philosophers. On that day mankind would, in Socrates's opinion, have a true republic.

As Reist explained to his Hillsdale students, "Socrates was a threat because he wanted to open people's minds to the possibility that they they may be wrong, that their teachers will be wrong and that the politicians may be wrong." Wise in his unwisdom, he suggested that the ring of invisibility was just a test. Those who were naive enough to believe that they could truly become invisible when it suited their purpose, were destined to become their own victims.

Roche was certainly not the first college president or important political figure to end up in such a tangled web of corruption. Leaders all the way up to the White House had difficulty owning up to the truth.

"The funny thing is Clinton got away with everything he did and the same people hounding George are the same people excusing Clinton," said June Roche. "I'm just devastated by what has happened and the way the conservative movement has turned on us."[160]

Lissa's decision to wait and break the news of her affair during the last hours of her life added to the confusion. The fact that so many people including the board of trustees appeared to believe IV's story over George Roche's denial says a good deal about IV's handling of the media. In the spirit of Machiavelli, he not only toppled his father, he pushed him out of the Midwest. Reduced to the occasional family visit, Roche would be lucky if his name remained on the recreational sports facility where IV worked.

By convincing people he'd been cuckolded, IV remained an object of sympathy and a hero to those who believed his father was a latter-day Gyges. But what happens to the spirit of a man who becomes invisible after his wife has talked of suicide?

As the presidential search committee reviewed potential candidates such as Whitewater special prosecutor Ken Starr, the entire Hillsdale community pulled together toward an uncertain future. While admissions applications were off 10 percent, vice president John Cervini was proud to announce that gift giving was unaffected by the fall of the House of Roche. "We are going to report a good year and we are going to balance the budget. The school is still going to be independent, not accept federal aid and not be politically correct. It's still going to be a fine, fine school.

"Academically there is no finer undergraduate liberal arts college in the country. We are what we say we are. We teach Western civilization, we teach American heritage. We have a real core of liberal arts courses that every student has to take irrespective of major. And I would say we have some of the finest undergraduate teachers in the country and they enjoy what they do."[161]

Clearly in that group was Dan York, the young anatomy and physiology instructor who had just moved with his wife Pia and their children to a beautiful old home on the edge of the campus. On a Friday night when cheers were going up from a student party down the block, the Yorks described some of the compelling reasons why they had come to Hillsdale. In the tradition of Ransom Dunn they believed this was a place where free inquiry made all the difference. While much had changed in the century and a half since the college had opened its doors, the Yorks knew anything was possible at Hillsdale. All you had to do was ask.

"In my last job at a liberal arts college in the Miami area," Dan told me in a high-ceilinged living room where peeling wallpaper suggested that remodeling was just around the corner for the happy new homeowners, "90 percent of the revenue came from tuition. We had faculty telethons where we called accepted applicants to try to convince them to enroll."

Uncomfortable with the concept of cold-calling a high school student and saying "Hello, this is Professor York calling from ... University," he decided that he hadn't gotten a Ph.D. to be a telemarketer.

There was also a little problem with crime in the Miami area. "We like the fact that Hillsdale is a safe place," Pia told me. "I was threatened at knifepoint one night in Miami when I went out to get my car."

One alternative for Dan was a tenure track job at a large multiversity. "When I was starting out I was warned by one professor at a large university that morphology was not the best way to get tenure. He took me aside and explained that in five years you have to bring in about $500,000 in grants or you don't get tenure."

Dan was advised against becoming a morphologist because a typical grant of, say $40,000, was a drop in the bucket. "Morphologists travel to museums looking at dead snakes. A professor of microbiology needs a centrifuge and a high powered lab spending $500 to $1,000 a day in reagents," he said. "It took me awhile to realize that the large universities are as much businesses as Wal-Mart or Penneys. They get their money through government grants."

At Hillsdale, Dan enjoys the "freedom to teach what I want and get so much more done. We have a secure endowment of several hundred million dollars. . . . Only 24 percent of the revenue is tuition generated. We don't have to do faculty telethons. There's an incredible system of donors nationally and worldwide. People can learn what they want and people can teach what they want to teach. It's run like a business by business people. There's no Peter Principle here. Faculty aren't running the show and that is one of the reasons it is working."

York has been able to pursue research interests that might have been beyond his reach at a larger university. He is studying why rhinoceros fertility is better in South Africa than the United States. Thanks to a new research center being built by Hillsdale in South Africa, he's been able to gather game data and collect rhinoceros dung for analysis. And, without worrying about government funding, he's also been able to do microbiology research. A pair of undergraduate student research assistants on one of these projects are receiving credit for assisting York on a scientific paper. "That doesn't happen at a big college."

There are many other reasons why the Yorks value this community. The Hillsdale Academy has been a godsend for their 10-year-old daughter. "The public school here in Hillsdale dropped its accelerated and gifted program. Kids showed up with major behavior problems. Our daughter was not doing her homework. The academy has good programs. They are going back to the basic foundation of education. They stress scholarship."

Of course the fishbowl atmosphere of small town living can be a bit of an annoyance for those who value their privacy. But the Yorks are touched by Hillsdale's sense of community. "If your water pipe bursts you have 10 people calling and asking if you need help," said Pia who teaches at the local branch of Jackson Community College.

York spoke about many of the wonderful benefits of a Hillsdale education at the October 1999 Shavano conference in Costa Mesa. It was the first time the couple had a chance to join one of these celebrity events. They loved it. "Lissa Roche was very upbeat at the Shavano and apologized for not getting together more," said Pia.

Dan York, one of the last people outside the Roche family to see Lissa alive, told me he noted nothing in her behavior that foreshadowed her death. He simply looked across the street Sunday morning October 17 and noticed Lissa walking up to Broadlawn with a book and a bowl of soup for Granaw. Sitting on a living room couch, Pia handed me a photo in a plastic holder. It was a shot of Lissa blowing a kiss to a freshly caught trout. Her baseball cap, t-shirt, healthy tan and smile were perfectly captured by the photographer, 15-year-old Nick York. Lissa had taken Nick and Jake Roche out to hone their angling skills.

Pia York appeared to be holding back tears as I looked at the time stamp on the photograph. It was taken on October 16, 1999, the day before Lissa died.

A few feet away was a small goldfish tank that had been brought to the Yorks following the divorce of George and June Roche. Inside were a pair of goldfish. "Dan," Lissa had explained while assigning custody of the two fish, "you are a biologist and we thought you would be interested in these."

As I walked up for a closer look, Pia York recalled the day the goldfish arrived. As we studied the tank, she spoke of the many pleasant times her son had spent with their Broadlawn neighbors. They had made him an important part of their extended family. Lissa and her father-in-law included him on outings, trips to museums and sporting events. Nick York, upstairs in his room doing his homework, had lost a good friend. It was after 11 P.M. when the Yorks walked me to the door of their home. Pia pointed to the goldfish swimming about in their tank. "These are the last two Roches," she said with a smile that masked the pain of a friend who misses Lissa every day.

It's Not Nearly as Bad as It Sounds

"Mostly I believe he was writing about his discovery of God—or maybe God's discovery of George. One day he looked up and saw the face of God and realized He had been there all along—in the people and the country he loved. There was something special between George and his Maker, something each of us must discover for himself. George has gone home now."

—A fictional Gibby Gregg, quoted in
George Roche III's novel *Going Home*

IN APRIL 2000 LARRY ARNN, the president of California's Claremont Institute, was named president of Hillsdale College. His inauguration was scheduled for September 9, with Supreme Court Justice Clarence Thomas delivering the main address. On May 13, 2000, IV married Akiko Tani in a ceremony at his mother's home. The couple honeymooned in Hawaii. June Roche flew to the islands to meet her new daughter-in-law's family. She traveled on a frequent flyer award from her ex-husband. Jake spent the summer in Colorado helping his father and Dean fix up their new home and chopping wood. On August 5 Margaret Roche ("Granaw") died in Montrose. She was buried next to her husband at Fort

Logan, Colorado. Later that month George Roche returned to Hillsdale for a brief visit. By the time he arrived his son IV and Akiko Tani had moved to Oregon. George V was now living in June Roche's basement. Weddings had resumed at the stone gazebo, reconsecrated by a local minister.

Hillsdale's prosecuting attorney, on the scene shortly after Lissa's death, said he had not received a request from the police to investigate the case. According to Hillsdale City Manager Tim Vagle the complete Lissa Roche autopsy was never released to protect the privacy of the woman who ended her career by bringing down the reign of her father-in-law. Both George and June Roche privately characterized the entire scandal as a Greek tragedy.

At the Hillsdale College May 13, 2000, commencement, an honorary doctorate was presented to speaker Paul Harvey who had last appeared at Hillsdale's 1965 graduation. There was no doubt in his mind that the school's brilliant students would lead Michigan and the nation in the years ahead: "It is entirely possible that a womb on this beautiful hillside one day will produce the Einstein who will reveal that empty space is not really empty after all....

"I shan't say more in praise of this campus. I'm going to save that for some soon broadcast when we have the entire nation listening.... Please, the myopic headlines are preoccupied with malfeasance, misfeasance, mistakes, because noise makes news, because one gunshot makes more noise than a thousand prayers, but that does not mean that it is more important. Don't let the headline writers rain on your parade....As Mark Twain is said to have said of the music of Richard Wagner, 'It's not nearly as bad as it sounds.'"[162]

Chronology of Events

1998

August—George Roche serves June Roche with divorce papers.

August—George invites his son IV and daughter-in-law Lissa Roche to move into Broadlawn.

1999

April—Roche divorce is final.

July—June and Jake Roche vacation in Colorado

July—June has surgery in Colorado, discovers she may have cancer.

August—June is diagnosed with Hodgkin's lymphoma; chemotherapy begins in Michigan.

September 8—Lissa abruptly resigns from Hillsdale College, announces she will divorce IV whom she suspects is having an extramarital affair.

September 8—Lissa arrives in California, calls IV, learns George is marrying Dean Hagan, whom he has been secretly dating for a year.

September 9—Lissa returns to Hillsdale.

September 10–11—Lissa and IV move out of Broadlawn and return to stone cottage down the street.

September 10–12—Lissa tries to talk Dean Hagan out of marrying George.

September 13—Dean and George marry. Lissa acts out at the wedding party, tells Dean she is marrying into "the most fucked-up family you will ever know."

September 14—Lissa reduces her office responsibilities.

October 11–12—Lissa, Dean, George III attend Shavano Institute conference in California. Lissa doesn't seem herself.

October 15—George tells Lissa he wants to annul his marriage to Dean.

October 16—Lissa takes her brother-in-law Jake and Nick York fishing.

Late October 16, early October 17—George becomes ill, is admitted to the Hillsdale Community Health Center emergency room in insulin shock.

October 17

Early hours—IV is called to the hospital by Dean Hagan. He returns home at 3 A.M., tells Lissa that his father and Dean Hagan have reconciled. Annulment plans are canceled. Lissa rushes to hospital, confronts Dean and is asked to leave by hospital staff following her outburst.

Morning—Lissa phones George shortly before 10 A.M., asks if the extended family can move back to Buena Vista, Colorado. George says this is impossible. Lissa threatens suicide. After hanging up, George calls his secretary Pat Loper, asks her to find IV and bring him home to Lissa.

10 A.M.—Loper drives to Jonesville and finds that IV is teaching a shooting class nearby. She drives IV to Broadlawn where Lissa is visiting with Granaw.

About 11 A.M.—Lissa and IV drive to the medical center. Lissa confronts George and Dean. Claims she has had a 19-year affair with George and that he has also had affairs with Hillsdale coeds.

Later that morning—IV drops Lissa off at home and returns to the hospital to ask his father if her allegations are true. George denies Lissa's allegations. IV leaves after being advised by Dean and medical staff to bring Lissa back to the hospital. IV obtains phone number for a crisis intervention team from the hospital staff.

12:30 P.M.—IV returns home to the stone cottage, 291 Hillsdale Street. Talks with Lissa and she asks him to drive eight doors to Broadlawn and check on Granaw. IV claims that at 12:30 he drives to Broadlawn, meets his father and Dean, turns around and immediately returns home. George, Dean confirm that they returned to Broadlawn about 12:30 P.M. but they deny seeing IV. According to Dean, Granaw supports this denial.

12:30 to 1:14 P.M.—During this time period, IV says he returned to the stone cottage, found Lissa missing and then noticed a rear gate to the house was left open. He claims he headed out through the back gate, found broken pine needles on the path leading down to the Slayton Arboretum where he discovered her body on the floor of a stone gazebo. Next to her was one of his guns, a .357. After examining the scene, he discovered the gun had been taken from a locked cabinet in their house. He says he concluded that she died of a self-inflicted gunshot wound.

1:14 P.M.—IV calls 911.

IV: "Hello, this is George Roche. My wife just shot herself."

Dispatcher: "What's the address?"

IV: "291 Hillsdale."

Dispatcher: "We have a female victim of suicide."

Patrolman: "10-4."

Dispatcher: "Get a police car over there."

Patrolman: "Is this a private residence or a grocery store?"

Dispatcher: "Private residence."

Police arrive at scene, begin investigation, question IV who asks to speak to Robert Blackstock, Hillsdale provost. After speaking with Blackstock, IV elects not to tell the police about Lissa's allegations of a lengthy love affair with his father. He reports to Blackstock about the alleged affair on the way home from the police station.

October 20—Visitation to Lissa's remains at Van Horn-Eagle Funeral Home.

October 27—George and Dean Hagan leave for honeymoon in Hawaii.

October 27—IV meets with Hillsdale College vice president Ron Trowbridge, reveals Lissa's charges of an affair with his father. Trowbridge notifies trustees, who schedule an emergency meeting of their prudential committee.

October 28—George and Dean cut short their honeymoon to return home. They remain in the Detroit area.

November 1—Trustees place George on a leave of absence.

November 10—Roche denies charges of affair with Lissa at a full meeting of the board of trustees. He and Dean leave for Colorado.

November 12—*National Review* publishes interview with IV revealing Lissa's allegations of a 19-year affair with George. IV does not mention Lissa's allegations that George was also sleeping with coeds. He also does not mention George's denials of Lissa's charges.

November 15—Board announces George's retirement. Robert Blackstock is named interim president of Hillsdale College.

November 17—Police investigation continues. Authorities ask IV why he didn't tell them about Lissa's charges of an affair with George during the initial investigation. No fingerprints are found on IV's .357, or the locked gun cabinet where the weapon was stored. No fingerprints are taken from the spent bullet, the unused bullets or the speedloader. Police do not complete gunpowder residue test on samples taken from hands of Lissa and IV. Gun cabinet keys are not accounted for in the physical evidence taken from the death scene by police. There is no police search of the terrain adjacent to the incident site.

November 29—Hillsdale Police Department releases its file concluding that Lissa's death is a suicide. Police department photographs and a three-page detailed written examination of the autopsy are not released.

2000

January—George and Dean relocate permanently to Colorado, joined by Granaw.

April 5—Larry Arnn is named the new president of Hillsdale College.

May 13—IV marries Akiko Tani at his mother's home in Hillsdale.

September 9—Larry Arnn is inaugurated as president of Hillsdale College. Supreme Court Justice Clarence Thomas delivers the main address.

Excerpts from the
Hillsdale Police Department Report

November 29, 1999

TO: Requesters of complete files
Hillsdale Police Department
Case #99-11397

RE: Freedom of Information Act Request
Lissa Roche's suicide

Attached is a copy of the entire Hillsdale City Police Department file regarding the Lissa Roche suicide, with certain redactions, for privacy reasons. Due to their graphic nature, Police Department photographs will not be released, nor will the 911 tape be released. A copy of that tape may be reviewed at the Police Department. Finally, the comprehensive summary of the Lucas County Coroner's report is included, however, a three-page detailed written examination of that autopsy will not be released....

Tim Vagle
City Manager

REPORT OF PATROLMAN RANDY CASLER:

While in the station 911 dispatched myself and officer Gaskell to 291 Hillsdale Street on a call of a suicide victim at that location. The date of this incident is 10.17.99 with the call being received at 13:14:22. The call was placed by George Roche IV from 291 Hillsdale Street....

The content of the call was stated as that George Roche IV had called and stated that his wife had shot herself. 911 dispatched (sic) advised him that they would contact the police and the ambulance and get them enroute. Roche then stated that he was going to get his wife and the phone call was ended.

911 was requested shortly thereafter to make a return call and to get better information as to the residence. George Roche IV was contacted and they maintained him on the phone until my arrival.

When I arrived with the caller in my car after having picked him up at Hillsdale Street and Barber Drive, I was directed to pull up to the first gate opening of the arboretum. At the time of picking up the caller I was not aware of who he was.

We both entered the arboretum as he directed me to the gazebo structure. As I approached the structure I could see what appeared to be a female victim laying on the floor of the gazebo. Further observation was made and it was noted that there was a large amount of bright red blood near the victim's head. The victim was motionless. The victim's eyes were fixed open and the pupils were dilated. The head was turned to the victim's right and pointed in a westerly direction.

The victim was clothed in a white pair of tennis shoes with white socks. She also had on a pair of navy blue shorts with the words Hillsdale College printed on them. She also had on a white tee shirt type top. A watch was noted on the left wrist.

A stainless steel revolver was noticed on the victim's right side. This revolver was of a stainless steel color with rubber and wood grip combination. It appeared to be a Ruger make pistol with an approximately four-inch barrel. The barrel of the gun was pointed in a southwestern direction. It appeared that the gun was approximately one to two feet from the right hand of the victim.

A gray pillow was observed on the left side of the victim. This pillow was approximately three to four feet from the victim's left foot. The pillow appeared to be creased so as to have it stand like a tent with the angle portion up and pointed on the side towards the victim.

There was blood on the victim's right knee.

AMBULANCE RESPONSE:

The Reading EMS was called to the scene by 911 with Anita Magda and Kevin Murray arriving on the scene. Contact was made with them at the gazebo and they advised with the large amount of blood near the head and the open eyes with fixed pupils that the victim was expired. They were asked if they needed to make closer examination to determine life signs and if they did to attempt to not disturb the scene as much as possible. They stated that they did not need to check and were sure of that (sic) the victim was dead and that they recommended that the Medical Examiner be called to make that determination. The EMTs cleared the area and returned to there (sic) ambulance.

MEDICAL EXAMINER INFORMATION

Dr. Jon Herbener was the on-call Medical Examiner and he responded to the scene arriving at 14:07:04.

Dr. Herbener was the first person that entered the gazebo and he began his examination noting various blood spot locations. The gun was described as a Ruger GP100, .357 Magnum revolver bearing serial number 17387309.

The following jewelry was noted on the victim. A necklace, gold in color with a medallion coin type charm of St. Christopher. Two gold colored earrings of a loop design, one in each ear. One silver watch with clasp opened. This watch was of a "ESQ" brand or model. The time on the watch when it was checked was 3:32 P.M. which was accurate as checked against my watch. The date showing was the 16th.

CRIME SCENE INVESTIGATION:

The crime scene was processed by Deputy John Gessner and assisted by Deputy Rick Richardson.

This processing of the scene will be typed up as a report along with a crime scene layout. The evidence was processed by Deputy Gessner and was later turned over to Officer Casler. See Deputy Gessner's Supplement for full details.

CRIME SCENE PERSONNEL:

Sgt. John Kase (Scene Supervisor)
Detective Brad Martin
Officer Randy Casler (First Officer On Scene and Investigative Officer)
Officer Tom Gaskell (Second Officer On Scene)
Officer Steve Pratt
Sgt. Carl Albright
Deputy John Gessner (Crime Scene Tech.)
Deputy Rick Richardson
Dr. Jon Herbener (Medical Examiner)

Security around perimeter of the scene was provided by Head of College Security John Kalusniak and the Hillsdale College security detail.

ON SCENE INTERVIEW OF GEORGE ROCHE IV

Roche was first contacted at the intersection of Hillsdale Street and Barber Drive when I arrived in the area. He was noticed standing on the northeast corner of that intersection and waving me down while he held a portable telephone.

Roche came to the passenger window of the car and stated that "she was in the arboretum." I asked him where in the arboretum and he asked to get in my unit and he would show me. He got in the back seat and he directed me to drive to the first gate of the arboretum. We both exited the car (sic) he led me into the arboretum and at one point I could see the victim in the gazebo.

After examining the victim I went back to Roche to interview him. At that time I was not aware of who he was or his relationship to the victim. I was met by Officer Gaskell and advised him that we needed to get ahold of College Security as I felt that this was a college student and that we needed to attempt to identify her.

I turned to Roche and asked him how he happened to find the victim and he stated that the victim was his wife. I then asked him for his driver's license which he supplied. At this time I identified him as George Roche IV.

Roche was asked if he had seen the suicide. He stated that he had gone to his father's house to check on his grandmother at the suggestion of his wife. Roche stated that he did this and was gone for three to five minutes. He stated that when he returned he found his wife gone. He checked for her and she was not in the house. He then looked out back and saw the gate open. He said that the gate is always shut. He went to that gate and then descended into the arboretum and located his wife in the gazebo. He stated that he checked her and then went for help.

Roche was asked how old his wife was and he stated that she was 41. I asked him for her date of birth but he appeared to be shaken and could not provide me with that information.

I asked Roche if he recognized the weapon and he stated that the gun was his and that it was kept in a cabinet.

Roche then stated that he was concerned that his son would be arriving in the area as he lived at the Delta Tau Delta house and that he did not want him to see her. I advised him that I would take care of that. He then stated that he needed to call some people about the incident and requested to leave and return to his home.

OBSERVATION OF WEAPON:

At 3:30 P.M., the weapon was checked by Deputy Gessner and five live rounds were dumped from the cylinder of the revolver. These rounds were identified as R-P .38 Spl. Plus P, with hollow point bullets.

One spent casing was removed from the cylinder which was also identified as R-P .38 Spl. Plus P.

OBSERVATION OF CLOTHING:

The victim was wearing a pair of L. L. Bean tennis shoes that were white in color. White ankle socks were also noted. The victim had on navy blue shorts with "Hillsdale College" printed on them and also were bearing a Champion logo. Underneath these shorts were a white pair of "Jockey" briefs. The victim had on a white tee shirt, short sleeves. Underneath this shirt was a white spaghetti strap athletic type shirt. The victim was not wearing a brassier (sic). These observations were noted by myself and Dr. Herbener.

OBSERVATIONS OF VICTIM WOUND:

Lissa Roche's wound was observed by Dr. Herbener and a single entry wound was located on the right side of the head just above the ear. At this time no other wounds were readily observable.

PHOTOGRAPHS:

I began taking photographs shortly after my arrival on the scene. I took photographs of the victim from each opening of the gazebo. I also attempted a photograph of a footprint found on the north side of the gazebo. Two rolls of 12 exposure film were shot as well as a partial roll of 24 exposures.

Deputy Gessner also shot one roll of 36 exposures.

MISCELLANEOUS NOTES:

George Roche IV stated that his wife was right handed. He also advised that the gun cabinet was locked when he checked it.

Roche stated that his wife had been despondent for a while over family matters. When asked about these he stated that she was upset over a divorce and his fathers (sic) remarrying. Roche stated that she had mentioned that she would kill herself. While he was at the Hillsdale Community Hospital he asked for some help for his wife. He stated that he was provided with a telephone number for Lifeways or Community Mental Health and he showed me a piece of paper with the phone numbers on it.

ADDITIONAL INFORMATION:

Interviews with George Roche IV were conducted by Officer Gaskell and Detective Martin. See their supplements concerning this area.

Followup interviews will be conducted by Detective Martin.

Lissa Roche's body was removed from the scene by personnel from the Van Horn-Eagle Funeral Home under the supervision of Dr. John Herbener. Her body was taken to the Hillsdale Community Hospital Morgue where it was secured by Sgt. Kase until it was taken to the Lucas County Medical Examiners Office. This was arranged by Dr. Herbener.

Once the body was removed from the scene I remained there while a cleanup crew from the Hillsdale College sanitized the area. During this process I remained to observe the clean up for any possible evidence overlooked, none was found and the scene was cleared.

STATUS:

Case open for further investigation.

PATROLMAN GASKELL INVESTIGATION:

While at home on lunch, Ptm. Gaskell received a radio run from Central Dispatch to make contact at 291 Hillsdale St. reference a suicide victim. Ptm. Gaskell asked Central if this radio run was reference a suicide victim or a suicide in progress. Central responded it was a suicide victim at 291 Hillsdale St. As Ptm. Gaskell was responding, Ptm. Casler advised it was in the arboretum. Ptm. Gaskell arrived, he observed Ptm. Casler's patrol vehicle and REMS ambulance parked on Barber St. in front of the first gate to the arboretum. Ptm. Gaskell responded to a gazebo made out of stone and wood located near the west end of the arboretum. While enroute to the gazebo, Ptm. Gaskell passed a white male subject standing away from the gazebo with a cordless phone in his hand, later identified as George Charles Roche IV. Once at the gazebo, Ptm. Gaskell observed a white female subject lying on the floor of the gazebo face up. The top of her head was facing north. Her head was lying in a large pool of bright red blood and her pupils were fixed. Lying about two feet west of the body was a silver in color, 4-inch barrel hand gun with rubber hand grips pointed in a southwest direction.

Upon checking with Ptm. Casler and REMS personnel, Anita Magda and Kevin Murray, it was determined the female subject was deceased. Ptm. Gaskell assisted in securing the scene until Sgt. Kase and Dr. John Herbener, Medical Examiner, arrived on the scene. Dr. Herbener requested the (sic) Roche be located and asked if he would submit to a gun powder residue procedure to be conducted by Deputy John Gessner, evidence tech. Ptm. Gaskell left the scene and responded to 291 Hillsdale St., Roche's residence.

INTERVIEW OF ROCHE:

Ptm. Gaskell arrived and observed George Roche IV, George Roche III and a white female, later identified by George IV as a mutual friend of his and Lissa. The female had a background in counseling (sic) but had arrived after the body had been found. Ptm. Gaskell asked George IV if he would submit to the gunpowder residue test and George IV agreed. George IV advised he had shot a muzzle loader type gun yesterday, but he had washed his hands several times since.

Ptm. Gaskell asked George IV which funeral home would handle the arrangements and George IV requested Van Horn-Eagle. George IV asked if they handled cremations? Ptm. Gaskell responded they do, and George IV checked with George III. George III responded that was fine. George IV agreed to be transported to the station, but requested to stop by Burger King on the way. He advised he has stomach problems and when he becomes upset especially by stress, he has to eat. Ptm. Gaskell transported him to Burger King where he ordered a Whooper Jr. (sic), with cheese and a sprite.

During the transport, George IV advised he had known Lissa for 25 years and married for 22 years. But during the last month, Lissa had really changed. Lissa had become very flighty and depressed. Lissa was very depressed about George III's divorce and remarrying so quickly. Both Lissa and George IV were having a difficult time with their son, George, attending Hillsdale College. Lissa was also upset about George IV's 15-year-old brother, George[163], who was attending Hastings Public School and living with George IV's sister in Hastings. The brother's academic performance at Hillsdale College had dropped since his parents' divorce and his father remarried.

Dr. Lusty was Lissa's physician. The only medication Lissa was taking was diet pills and birth control pills.

George IV advised Lissa had left him for a couple of days earlier this month but she had moved back home and they were attempting to work out their problems.

George IV advised numerous family problems had occurred since the early morning hours. George IV said the last time he saw Lissa living, she asked him to go check on his grandmother, who was staying with George III at his residence. George IV responded to 189 Hillsdale St., checked on his grandmother, who was ok, and he returned to 291 Hillsdale St. Upon entering his residence, he found no one home and started to check the residence. He looked out the back of the house, and saw the gate to the arboretum open. He went down to the arboretum and located Lissa lying on the floor of the gazebo with a pool of blood around her head. Also, lying close to her right hand was a gun, which belonged to him. George IV entered the gazebo, kneeled down next to her and reached across her body to check the carotid pulse. George IV did not locate one. Thus he ran back up to the house and called for help.

George IV advised he was right handed.

While at the station waiting for Deputy Gessner, George IV made numerous phone calls. The first call George IV made was to a department head. George advised this subject he would not be able to teach the additional classes next semester and then George IV told the department head about Lissa shooting herself. Another phone call George IV made, he congratulated the subject first about an event, and then told them about Lissa shooting herself.

Ptm. Gaskell attempted to interview George IV about the day's activities but was interrupted by Sgt. Kase and Det. Martin's phone call. Det. Martin requested a written statement be obtained as soon as possible, as he was enroute to the station. Ptm. Gaskell asked George IV for a written statement, and George IV responded, he wanted to talk to an attorney first. George IV mentioned the name of Jack Barker and started to look up his phone number. Ptm. Gaskell mentioned Bob Blackstock, a Hillsdale College administration official who had practiced law, who had been at the scene. George IV requested to speak with him. Blackstock was located and responded to the scene. Ptm. Gaskell met Blackstock in the lobby of the department and advised him. Blackstock advised since taking the college position, he had placed his law license in escrow and was not a practicing attorney. George and Blackstock spoke in private in the main hallway, and upon returning to the dispatch area, George IV stated he would be willing to complete a written statement. George IV completed a statement which was reviewed by Blackstock. At George IV's request, a copy of the statement was given to both George IV and Blackstock. This statement was given to Det. Martin.

OFFICER'S OBSERVATIONS

Ptm. Gaskell was with George IV from approximately 1425 hours thru 1730 hours. Never once did George IV cry even while making numerous phone calls from the station. George IV never showed outward signs of being emotionally upset over Lissa' death. But when George was asked Lissa's date of birth, George responded February 17 or maybe February 27, 1957. Lissa's date of birth was 2/17/58. George said Lissa had never talked about suicide until today.

STATUS:

Open pending further investigation

Follow-up/Suicide/Death Investigation

INFORMATION:

While off duty in Jackson, Michigan, the undersigned received a page from Central Dispatch. The time of the page was approximately 1319 hours. Subsequently, after learning of the type of call, the undersigned spoke with both Officer Casler and Officer Gaskell. They advised that for the time being, they had additional help enroute and that the undersigned's immediate response was not necessary.

At approximately 1550 hours, the undersigned first responded to the station to check with the investigating officers. The undersigned responded to the dispatch area and observed George Roche IV, Robert Blackstock and Officer Gaskell. George Roche IV was making a written statement and stopped as the undersigned entered and greetings were conducted. The undersigned immediately noted that George's emotional state was controlled. His face was somewhat pale in color but his composure was normal. He was not crying or emotionally upset. The undersigned quickly learned that the scene investigation was still ongoing and at that time, the undersigned left the station and drove to the scene:

CONTACT WITH INVESTIGATORS AT SCENE:

At approximately 1600 hours, the undersigned drove to the Hillsdale College Arboretum and first observed Security Director John Kalusniak and Vice President Rich Pewe. They directed the undersigned to park just inside the gate area and from there, the undersigned walked to the gazebo area. The undersigned observed Dr. John Herbener, Prosecutor Neal Brady, Deputy John Gessner, Sgt. John Kase and Officer Randy Casler. The undersigned was briefed by both Sgt. Kase and Officer Randy Casler. After receiving the basic details, the undersigned spoke briefly with Officer Casler concerning the need at that point to conduct a search of the victim's residence. The search would be for signs of foul play and/or a suicide note.

RETURN TO STATION/CONSENT TO SEARCH:

After speaking with Officer Casler, the undersigned returned to the station for the purpose of gaining consent to search the residence and to gather equipment. The undersigned spoke briefly with George Roche IV concerning the need to search his residence. George stated that he understood. Also, Robert Blackstock acknowledge (sic) the need for the search. The undersigned pointed out that George had the right to refuse the search. At that time, both George and

Mr. Blackstock stated that he would sign a consent form and allow a search of both his and the victim's residence. They both then signed a "permission to search" form. The time was approximately 1620 hours.

INVESTIGATION AT HEALTH CENTER:

Prior to staring a search at the Roche residence, the undersigned drove to the Health Center to make contact with Dr. Herbener and Sgt. Kase. The undersigned arrived at the Health Center at approximately 1625 hours and immediately met with Dr. John Herbener. He was asked for his initial assessment of the investigation. Dr. Herbener advised that it was his opinion that the death was a suicide. After a brief conversation with Dr. Herbener, the undersigned then made contact with Sgt. Kase who was guarding the body inside the Hospital Morgue. The undersigned spoke with Sgt. Kase while he waited for a representative from Van Horn-Eagle to arrive and transport the body. At approximately 1645 hours, John Barrett of Van Horn arrived and took possession of the body. Both the undersigned and Sgt. Kase then left the hospital and returned to the station. The undersigned found that George Roche IV was still at the station and advised him that a search of his residence had not yet been done. George stated that he needed to check on his grandmother and would then meet the undersigned at the residence.

SEARCH OF RESIDENCE:

At approximately 1655 hours, the undersigned and Sgt. Kase arrived at the Roche residence to conduct the search there. Upon our arrival the following subjects were present there; George Roche III, Jeffrey Daglow and Muriel Roche. Also present was another young man and a middle age woman

who at this time have not yet been identified. The undersigned
and Sgt. Kase did a walk through the residence. The undersigned noted that the residence was very clean and neat. The
undersigned check (sic) areas such as tables and desk tops for
signs for a suicide note. None were found. After concluding
a brief walk through of the residence and noting no signs of
foul play, George Roche IV arrived and volunteered to go
over his actions again leading up to the discovery of the body,
(see interview below).

SEARCH OF EXTERIOR/GATE AND PATHWAY:

After speaking with George briefly in reference to his
actions and observations, the undersigned and Sgt. Kase then
checked the rear yard of the residence, including the gate to
the arboretum. The undersigned noted that the gate was closed
and had an older style latch system. It also had a locking hasp
above the latch which appeared in operable (sic). The undersigned noted that when the gate swung to the closed position,
the latch would not "catch" into the closed position on it's
(sic) own. In an earlier interview with George Roche IV, he
stated that he had noted that the gate was not latched shut
and that he himself always made sure that it was. In checking
the arboretum area on the other side of the gate, the undersigned noted a very narrow pathway which was covered with
fallen pine needles. An area of pine needles near the gate
seemed to be disturbed. However, in following the path down
toward the gazebo and to a series of stone steps, the undersigned did not see any areas where the pine needles appeared
to be disturbed. In the earlier interview with George IV, he
stated that after finding the gate unlatched, he checked the
path and steps which led to the lower gazebo and observed
areas in which the pine needles appeared to be disturbed. For

that reason, he continued down the path toward the gazebo, looking for his wife, Lissa.

SEARCH IN RESIDENCE, CONTINUED:

At approximately 1710 hours, the undersigned and Sgt. Case returned inside the residence and continued the search. The undersigned's attention was drawn to a laptop computer which was located inside a room of the house which was being used as an office. Jeff Daglow, a friend of the Roches, stated that the room was used by Lissa as her office. The undersigned looked closely at the computer and located the power button. The computer was turned on and the main working area was visible. The undersigned did not note any files which were visibly displayed and were dated with the present date. After looking at the main working area briefly, the undersigned decided to shut the computer down and allow someone more knowledgeable (sic) to examine it more closely. The computer was shut down at approximately 1720 hours, 10/17/99.

CONCLUSION OF SEARCH/TABULATION SIGNED:

The undersigned concluded the search at approximately 1722 hours. A tabulation was completed and signed, noting the laptop computer which was being taken. Consent search tabulation was completed and signed at 1725 hours....

INTERVIEW WITH GEORGE ROCHE IV:

While at the victim's residence conducting a consent search, her husband, George Roche IV, returned there and volunteered to once again go over his observations prior to discovering his wife in the gazebo area. He stated that earlier in the day, he and his wife had been inside the residence talking in the living room concerning her despondency. After a short while, she asked him to go check on his grandmother who was staying at his father's residence. George stated that he then left his wife alone in the house and was gone for no more than five minutes. When he returned, he did not find his wife inside. He observed that the back door was open. Upon checking the back gate which leads to the college arboretum, he found that the latch was in the open position. Knowing that he himself always made sure it was closed, he opened the gate and checked further into the arboretum. He noticed that some of the pine needles were disturbed along the pathway which leads to the main gazebo and continued looking for Lissa until he found her laying in the gazebo. He returned to his residence to call 911. George stated that he noted that his gun cabinet was locked and upon checking further, the pistol case was also locked. However, the gun was missing. Also, he noted that one of his speed loaders had been emptied.

OBSERVATIONS:

The undersigned noted that George Roche IV displayed a "controlled" emotional state. He never became "upset" nor did he cry. His face appeared to be pale in color and he did appear to be disturbed.

OTHER OBSERVATIONS:

Upon arrival at the Roche residence, 291 Hillsdale, the undersigned also was greeted by Dr. Roche, (George Roche III). The undersigned noted that his face was pale in color. The undersigned shook his hand and noted that his hand felt warm and moist.

FINGERPRINTS:

On October 19, 1999, at approximately 12:20 P.M., the undersigned fingerprinted the victim, Lissa Jackson Roche. The fingerprinting was conducted prior to cremation at the Paschal burial vault in Hudson MI. Although the undersigned was assisted by two employee's (sic) of the Van Horn-Eagle Funeral Homes, there was difficulty in obtaining good, quality, inked impressions. Impressions were obtained and at 1241 hours on the same date, the print card was signed by the undersigned and the two representatives from Van Horn-Eagle....

STATUS:

Open-pending further investigation. Note—At this time, the death appears to be "self-inflicted."

Bradley J. Martin
Detective
Hillsdale Police Department

INFORMATION:

On 11/09/99, the undersigned met with Dr. Roche at his residence. Dr. Roche was asked to give an account of what had happened on October 17, 1999, starting with emergency visit to the hospital. Dr. Roche gave the following account:

He stated that very early in the morning at approximately 1:00 A.M., he suffered a diabetic reaction and became very ill. While being cared for by his new wife, Dean Roche, his son, IV was called to the house. Dr. Roche stated that later, at approximately 3:00 A.M., he remembered being treated inside one of the trauma rooms at the Health Center. There, he recalled the first incident in which Lissa visited with him inside the trauma room and was visibly irritated and irrational. Dr. Roche stated that Lissa was argumentative with both he and his wife, Dean. Approximately 7 hours later, after being admitted to one of the hospital rooms, Dr. Roche recalled another visit in which Lissa became upset again and made accusations towards him in the presence of both IV and Dean. Dr. Roche stated that Lissa claimed that he and she had been having an affair and that Dean did not know what type of person she had married. Dr. Roche stated that Lissa was acting very irrational and upset. Again, Lissa left and then a short while later, Dr. Roche received a telephone call from Lissa in which she indicated that she was going to kill herself. Dr. Roche did not speak with Lissa very long and immediately afterwards, notified Pat Loper at home and requested her to contact IV who was in Jonesville at the time. Dr. Roche stated that after the confrontation inside the hospital room and after IV and Lissa left, IV returned and asked if him (sic) if they really did have an affair. Dr. Roche stated that he denied to George that they had an affair. Dr. Roche then explained to the undersigned that Lissa's accusations were untrue and that they had not had an affair of any sorts. He explained that Lissa had been experiencing problems in her marriage and with her son and because of this, was under an emotional strain.

Dr. Roche indicated that due to his illness, he was somewhat confused about the course of events that early morning and day. However, he believed that Lissa's phone call was after her earlier visits.

When asked what time he arrived home from the hospital that day, Dr. Roche stated that he was not sure and that his wife Dean might know.

INTERVIEW WITH MRS ROCHE (Dean):

After speaking with Dr. Roche, the undersigned spoke with Dean Roche, the Dr.'s new wife. Dean stated that during Lissa's visits on October 17th., ds(sic) 1999, she showed signs of being irrational and unstable. However, she herself did not hear Lissa threaten to kill herself. When asked what time she and Dr. Roche arrived home from the hospital, Dean stated she believed it was approximately 12:30 P.M. When asked how it was that they heard about Lissa's death, Dean stated that a friend, Mrs. Angell, arrived at the house and told them that afternoon shortly after Lissa's body was discovered. Both Dr. Roche and Mrs. Roche were asked to prepare written statements at their earliest convenience.

LAB REPORT:

On or about Thursday, November 11, 1999, the undersigned received a lab report which indicated that there were no identifiable fingerprints found on the weapon in this case.

STATUS:

Open-pending follow-up Interview with George Roche IV.

INFORMATION:

On 11/19/99, the undersigned conducted a follow-up interview with George Roche IV. The interview was conducted at approximately 1:30 P.M.

George was asked how it was that Lissa gained access into the locked cabinet and retrieved the gun. He stated that both she and their son had keys to the gun cabinet which were kept on their key rings. When asked if Lissa was familiar with hand-guns, George replied that she had been shooting with him on prior occasions but he did not believe she had ever shot that particular gun.

George was then asked why it was that he did not divulge the alleged affair between Lissa and his father on the day of her death. He replied that after speaking with Robert Black-stock, he thought that the affair was something he did not wish to reveal at that time.

George was asked to give an account again concerning how it was that he found Lissa in the Arboretum. He stated that upon returning home from checking on his grandmother, he found that Lissa was gone and that the back, kitchen door was open. He started walking toward the gate and from a dis-tance, he could see that the gate was open, (not latched). He walked through the gate and observed that the pine needles were disturbed on the path which led toward the gazebo. The undersigned asked him to point out what he was talking about concerning the pine needles and at that time, showed him pic-tures taken of the trail and steps which led to the gazebo. George looked at the photos and then pointed out what he described as "impressions" in the needles, or areas in which it appeared to him that someone had walked on top of the needles. This caused him to start down the path toward the gazebo. Before reaching the gazebo, he could see that Lissa was inside and laying down. As he approached her, he could see blood on the front of her blouse and the gun laying on the floor of the gazebo.

George then was asked about the altercation at the hospi-tal and the events which led to the altercation. He stated that at approximately 10:30 A.M., he was contacted by Pat Loper while he was prepairing (sic) for an outdoor class in Jonesville.

He stated that Pat told him that Lisa (sic) had just spoken with his father over the telephone and that she was threatening to kill herself. George agreed to return to his father's residence with Pat. Upon his arrival, he met Lissa there at the Broadlawn residence. He pointed out that Lissa had been there, caring for his grandmother while his father and Dean were at the hospital. George stated that he asked Lissa to step outside so that they could talk. He noticed at that time that Lissa appeared "fine." He then told her that he had just been told by Pat Loper about her threats to kill herself. George stated that Lissa then became very upset and insisted they go to the hospital. George stated that they arrived at the hospital at approximately 11:00 A.M. to 11:15 A.M. During their trip to the hospital, Lissa repeated her threats to kill herself. They arrived at the hospital and then went up to his father's room. Once inside, Lissa started a confrontation, she openly spoke of the affair between she and his father. George stated that after the confrontation at the hospital, both he and she returned home. At their residence, they talked more and then George returned to the hospital. He made contacts with one of the nurses and with Dr. Panchell concerning Lissa's threat to kill herself. He then returned home and found Lissa sitting in front of the fireplace. They talked a short while and then Lissa asked George to return to Broadlawn to check on his grandmother. George stated that he did and that upon his arrival at Broadlawn, he met his father and Dean who were just returning home from the hospital. George stated that he thought that the time might have been sometime near 12:30 P.M. Upon questioning that time, George said that it may have been later than 12:30 P.M. He stated that he was gone for only 5 minutes or so and that he returned home to check on Lissa. Upon his arrival, he found that she was not there.

George was then asked if Lissa had been taking any type of tranquilizers. He stated she had only been taking diet type pills and birth control. He added that she may have had some over the counter sleeping pills like Tylenol PM. However, she had not been taking any tranquilizers.

INVESTIGATION RESULTS AS OF 11/22/99:

As of this date, George Roche's IV's initial statement in which he said that Lissa had been threatening to commit suicide that day has been cooberated (sic) by his father, Dr. Roche. Lissa had threatened to take her life to both Dr. Roche and to her husband, George Roche IV. Also, according to Dean Roche, Lissa was in a very distressed state of mind. Although an official autopsy report has not yet been received, it has been said that the autopsy revealed nothing which would suggest homicide. Dr. Herbener's investigation at the scene caused him to conclude that the death was due to a self inflicted gun shot wound to the head. As of 11/22/99, it is still the opinion of the undersigned that the death occurred as the result of a "self inflicted gun shot wound to the head."

NOTE—GUN POWER RESIDUE TEST:

The FBI was requested (by the Hillsdale Police Department) to analyze the gun powder residue swabs which were taken from both the victim and George Roche IV on the day of the victim's death (the gunpowder residue test was administered to IV's hands twice). The FBI has declined to conduct the test stating that they no longer conduct such tests due to the lack of evidence they provide. A list of private labs has been obtained and hopefully, in the near future, the swabs can be analyzed.

CONTACT WITH VICTIM'S SISTER, LAURA JACKSON:

On Monday, November 22nd, at approximately 3:30 P.M., the undersigned received a return phone call from the victim's twin sister, Laura Jackson. Early in the investigation, the undersigned had received her telephone number from Mrs. Roche. Several messages were left on Laura's answering machine. Laura apologized for not returning the undersigned's official call and advised that it has obviously been a difficult time. The undersigned explained to Laura that her input was important and then asked her if she had any suspicions in the case. Laura stated that she did not and that she, along with the rest of her family, felt confident that her sister did commit suicide.

STATUS:

Open-pending receipt of autopsy report/results of gun powder residue test.

Bradley J. Martin
Detective
Hillsdale Police Department

LUCAS COUNTY CORONER'S OFFICE, TOLEDO, OHIO

Case Summary On The Death of Lissa Roche. . . .

Opinion: It is my opinion that Lissa Roche died of gun-shot wound of the head. Manner of death: suicide-self-inflicted gunshot wound of the head, The Death Certification is to be signed by the Hillsdale County Coroner.

James R. Patrick M.D.
Coroner
Examination performed by Diane Scala-Barnett M.D.
Deputy Coroner (Lucas County)

STATEMENT OF GEORGE ROCHE IV, October 17, 1999

I was awakened at about 1:00 A.M. on Sunday morning. My step-mother was calling to ask for my help in a medical emergency. My father was having a diabetic insulin reaction. I called 911 for an ambulance and immediately drove to 189 Hillsdale St. My wife Lissa didn't awaken, so I didn't disturb her. I was at the hospital until after 3:00 A.M. When I got home, Lissa awakened and went briefly to the hospital. We slept until about 8:00 (A.M.) Sunday morning. Lissa went to Broadlawn to be with my grandmother, Margaret Roche. I prepared to meet a college class that I was teaching from 10:00–1:00. At 10:30 my father's secretary, Pat Loper interrupted my class to inform me that Lissa had threatened to commit suicide when talking with my father, who was still in the hospital. I returned to find Lissa at 189 Hillsdale St. She was very upset and insisted on going to the hospital. When we got to the hospital Lissa continued to be upset and she repeated her intention to commit suicide. We had been together for almost 25 years and she had never said anything like this before. After we returned to our home, she asked me to go back to the hospital to see my father. While at the hospital, I talked to a nurse and Dr. Panchel about Lissa's suicide threats. I also called a friend who used to work for Lifeways and she agreed to come see Lissa. When I returned home, she was sitting in front of our fireplace. We talked briefly and she asked me to run up the street to check on my grandmother before we talked further. I was gone less than five minutes. When I returned, our house was empty and the back door was open. I hurried into the Arboretum from our back yard to find Lissa dead in the gazebo. I ran back to our house to call 911 at about 1:05.

STATEMENT OF PATRICIA LOPER, October 25, 1999:

On Sunday October 17, I received a phone call from President Roche around 10 A.M. Dr. Roche indicated he received a call from Lissa Roche and she told Dr. Roche that she would kill herself. Dr. Roche asked me to go and find his son and Lissa's husband IV and tell him of Lissa's threat. (Dr. Roche was in the hospital and unable to go himself.) Dr. Roche told me I would find IV at a shooting class just east of Jonesville on US 12. Dr. Roche told me he was at Daglows and gave me the address (which I can't recall now). I went to Daglows and informed IV of Lissa's threat and he asked me to wait and give him a ride. I waited for IV and drove IV to his home in Hillsdale. I then returned to my home. I think I returned home at 11:00.

Lissa Roche's Letter of Resignation

Memorandum

Route To: Ron Trowbridge
Jon Corombos
Pat DuBois
Pat Loper
Tina Hess
Ellen Donohoe
John Cervini

From: Lissa Roche

Date: September 8, 1999

Re: Resignation

It grieves me to tell you that I am unable to continue as managing editor of *Imprimis* and the Hillsdale College Press. I am seeking a divorce from George IV for reasons I can't go into, and it seems best to get out of town immediately. I am sorry to leave you in the lurch like this.

I know that there will be a lot of talk about my sudden departure; please tell people that although it seems strange that I left in such a secretive manner it was simply to avoid a big fuss. You know me; I hate to be the object of attention. I have been such an object in the college community for many years now. I just want this to be as private as possible, and, most of all, I don't want to have to answer any questions. I will tell you that I am not leaving IV for someone else, since I know that will come up time and time again.

I will not be reachable by phone or mail. Tell Jill if any job termination paperwork has to be signed or W-2s forwarded later on, please mail to my sister, Laura Jackson. I will not be staying with her, but I will be in touch with her periodically. My final paycheck, if there is one, can be deposited as usual by auto deposit in my joint checking account with IV.

Pat and John should come by the house as soon as possible to pack up my computer and my files. The most important computer folder is the one on the desktop labeled URGENT! Things to Do.

Here is the status on the October *Imprimis*. We are very late! I sent the edited version of Steve Forbes remarks to him yesterday and gave him 7 working days to respond. I also gave Ron a Margaret Thatcher excerpt to get her approval on during the same period. And I e-mailed both to Robin at Myers and Associates so she could get started. Hopefully, she can read the files and the authors won't have many changes. If Thatcher says no, just do a photo section from the last 2 Shavanos. Be sure to take my name off the copyright section.

John, please keep calling the authors and pestering them to meet our deadline! (Steve Forbes secretary is Jacquie de Maria ... she may want you to deal with Steve's campaign manager.... There won't be much turnaround time for page proofs (you) may have to see what Cyril Scott can do for us in this emergency. You can fax to Christy Bych for her proofing, and Nancy Johnson always does a great job.

I did not start editing Bill Bennett s (sic) speech for the November *Imprimis* or Gleaves Whitney[164] for December. Pat check with Tom Curtis to make sure he has unedited drafts of both to do illustrations.

My files are arranged accordingly:

DESK
Left desktop wire basket items to go out in interoffice or U.S. mail

Right desktop wire basket items I am currently working on also see the phone message spiral book for important pending projects most important items are pending Imprimis issues

Left desk file drawer Office 98 disks/misc.

Left desk file drawer (bottom) reference articles on misc. subjects

Right desk file drawer (top)
pending (not urgent)
speeches that need to be written
Imprimis in press/upcoming/save
Freedom Library, including list of revisions that need to be made on next version
List-building/National Ad Campaign/Outreach

Right desk file drawer (bottom)
latest items re Broadlawn renovation
copies of recent POs
Champs 27—haven't done much with this so far;
need to transcribe some talks, get Richard s(sic)
from him, edit all and obtain authors approval, get ISBN# from Phyllis and send in Library of Congress form; do PO for Aatec. If mss. is ready by Nov, should have book by Jan., when John Cervini plans a mailing See hard copy file (on floor near desk) and disk files for Champs 26 to get an idea of what needs to be done
Budget files

CCA/Shavano files
Memo files

SET OF THREE FILE DRAWERS
Left file drawer (top)

Lost papers files Richard needs to be reminded of deadlines for editing chapters. By now the translators should have about 2/3s to 3/4s of what they need to work on. Tina pays them as they submit material. Richard has not been good about meeting deadlines. Hew HC manager needs to keep on him, and edit all chapters according to Chicago style manual.

various files for HC materials

Left file drawer (bottom)
empty files

Middle file drawer (top)
boilerplate
save temporary

<u>Please leave for George IV and make sure he knows where to find them:</u>

Middle file drawer (bottom)
personal bills to pay
checks
paystubs/canceled checks

Right file drawer (top)
personal, including important documents
(birth certificates, auto title, etc.)

Right file drawer (bottom)
personal

FLOOR AREA BY SET OF THREE FILE DRAWERS

Brown accordion file holds all paperwork related to Broad-lawn renovation, except the most recent items, which are in the right desk file drawer (bottom). All these should go to Rich P w.

CLOSET

misc. forms/stationery etc.
pink folder w/Lost Papers index hard copy/disk

HIRING

If you are looking for a replacement, here are some individuals to consider:

My first choice is Jon Corombos (someone else would replace him as Director of Seminars). We need someone with excellent editing skills and a feel for the Imprimis style. No one would be better than Jon.

Gleaves Whitney. Gleaves might be persuaded to go part-time in Governor s (sic) Office and do Imprimis only part-time from Lansing. Our circulation of nearly one million and the prospect that he might be the next president of Hillsdale College ought to be pointed out to him. Joe or Jon could then take on responsibility for doing Champions, Freedom Library, etc. Ron could handle all correspondence, financial details, list-building, etc. Or J.R. Avery in Mishawaka or Jack Koller could be hired as assistant managing editor and do all the extra stuff.

If you decided to interview other candidates, check with Stan Evans, Adam Meyerson, Fred Barnes, Rich Lowry, John

Fund and Tom Bray about their recommendations.

Remind the new editor that I tended to rewrite almost every Imprimis issue from top to bottom, while still trying to retain the unique style of the author. Every sentence needs crafting, sometimes over and over again. Often, material at end would move to beginning or vice versa. I also filled in many missing factual and philosophical points, and did a lot of fact-checking. Many authors are wrong, even about their own bios! I also made a lot of changes on page proofs that tightened up grammar, etc. Stick to Wall Street Journal style (not Hillsdale Magazine style, Chicago style, etc.)

Most of our authors have no problem with heavy editing. See permission letters in Imprimis issues folder on computer for samples of how to explain what editor has done.

HERBERT SWOPE

As you know, at John's suggestion, I have been helping Herbert Swope with his memoirs. He has final hard copies of the chapters we have completed (not many). What he doesn t (sic) have is hard copies of the unedited chapters (very rough) just unedited transcripts of some of our conversations) or disk copies of everything. Please send him everything with a note of apology for my being unable to help further: I have resigned, I can t (sic) continue for personal reason, etc. Please remember he is elderly and will be quite upset. This will probably kill off the project.

Sorry I can't be there to help. Will miss you dearest friends.

—Lissa Roche

George Roche's Farewell Letter

November 9, 1999

Dear Friends:

Knowing that the passing years brought ever closer the time of my departure from Hillsdale, I had always wondered how to say goodbye. Now the time has come.

In the grief and confusion surrounding the tragedy of Lissa's death, statements have been made that tarnish her memory. I must address those statements before I say goodbye. The details of my family's life should not be publicly discussed. Let it suffice to say that Lissa was a dear daughter to me for the last quarter century. She was one of the most wonderful co-workers that I have ever known. In my frequently unhappy and dysfunctional marriage, Lissa often functioned as a surrogate mother to my children. She loved and cared for the entire Roche family. Lissa and I were co-workers, close family, dearest friends and best buddies. We shared an immense emotional attachment. I would gladly do anything to bring her back to us, but, before God, I deny any improper relationship with my dear daughter Lissa.

I say this for her memory, not for mine. Once such allegations are loose in the world, they take on a life of their own, no matter how false. Many of my friends know and believe the truth. To them I give my love and deep appreciation. For those who relish the details of an imaginary scandal which so unjustly injures my family and Lissa's memory, I ask God's mercy.

In any case, it is time to leave Hillsdale. I am nearly 65 years old and no longer have a wish to continue. As I leave, I want to thank my many, many friends and co-workers. Together we built a wonderful school, a wonderful dream. We showed the way. We proved it could be done. Now that task is still in your hands. Hold the torch high. Show the world what courage, integrity and values can still mean, even in a badly corrupted world.

For my part, I shall always remember the friends and the work with deep pride. I will also remember the good times and the wonderful friends of Hillsdale. You will always be in my thoughts and prayers.

All my best,

George Roche

Notes

<small>INTRODUCTION</small>

1. Author's interview with Kay Cosgrove, April 1, 2000.

2. Board of Trustees meeting, May 1963.

3. Donald J. Phillips, Board of Trustees Report, June 1964.

4. Author's interview with John Willson, March 27, 2000.

5. Author's interview with Arlan Gilbert, March 12, 2000.

6. *Hillsdale College Catalog 1999–2000,* p. 75.

7. Arlan Gilbert, *The Permanent Things,* Hillsdale, 1998, pp. 175–176.

8. Gilbert, *The Permanent Things,* p. 209.

9. Ibid., p 211.

10. Ibid., p 211.

11. Ibid., p. 212.

12. Arlan Gilbert, *Historic Hillsdale College,* Hillsdale, 1991, p. 130.

13. *Detroit News,* December 26, 1999.

14. Ibid.

15. Author's interview with Dr. John Reist, March 26, 2000.

<small>CHAPTER 1</small>

16. Robert G. Anderson, "George and Me," privately published essay, 1999.

17. Ibid.

18. Ibid.

19. Author's interview with June Roche, March 13, 2000.

20. Ibid.

21. Anderson, "George and Me."

22. William P. Barrett, "Unique Selling Proposition," *Forbes,* May 17, 1999.

23. George Roche III, *A Reason for Living,* Regenery Gateway: Washington, D.C., p. 130. The story of Roche Jr.'s illness is thinly fictionalized in this book.

24. Ibid., pp. 67–68.

25. George Roche III, letter to Ed Quillen in *Colorado Central Magazine,* January 2000, p. 10.

26. George Roche, *One by One,* Hillsdale, 1990, p. 24.

27. Ibid.

28. Author's interview with Dorothy Roman, April 21, 2000.

29. Ibid.

30. Author's interview with June Roche, March 13, 2000.

31. Author's interview with Dorothy Roman, April 21, 2000.

32. George Roche III, *Legacy of Freedom,* Hillsdale, 1973, p. 56.

33. Author's interview with June Roche, March 13, 2000.

34. Gilbert, *Permanent Things,* p. 219.

35. Author's interview with June Roche, March 13, 2000.

36. Author's interview with anonymous friend of George Roche III, Spring 2000.

37. Author's interviews with Arlan and Carolyn Gilbert, March 12 and 13, 2000.

38. Ibid.

39. Barrett, "Unique Selling Proposition."

40. Author's interview with John Willson, March 27, 2000.

41. Ibid.

42. Author's interview with June Roche, March 13, 2000.

43. Anderson, *George and Me.*

44. Ibid.

45. "HEW Warns of Aid Cutoff," *Hillsdale Magazine,* January 1978.

46. George Roche, *In the First Place,* p. 6.

47. Author's interview with anonymous friend of George Roche III, Spring 2000.

48. "HEW Warns of Aid Cutoff."

49. Author's interview with anonymous friend of George Roche

III, Spring 2000.

50. Barrett, "Unique Selling Proposition," *Forbes*, May 17, 1999.

51. Roche, *One by One*, pp. 109–123.

CHAPTER 2

52. Anderson, "George and Me."

53. Author's interview with June Roche, March 13, 2000.

54. Author's interview with Arlan Gilbert, August 20, 2000.

55. Ibid.

56. Author's interview with John Andrews, April 26, 2000.

57. Ibid.

58. George Roche III, *Going Home*, Ottawa, Ill., 1986, p. 10.

59. Author's interview with Ed Quillen, March 21, 2000.

60. Author's interview with John Andrews, April 26, 2000.

61. Author's interview with Arlan Gilbert, August 20, 2000.

CHAPTER 3

62. Keith Windschuttle, *The Killing of History*, San Francisco, 2000, p. ix.

63. Roche, *One by One*, p. 90.

64. George Roche, *The Fall of the Ivory Tower*, Washington D.C., 1994, p. 209.

65. *Parents' Handbook and Directory Hillsdale*, 1999, p. 16.

66. Emily Eakin, "God and Man at Hillsdale," *Lingua Franca*, September 1996.

67. George Roche, *Parents Handbook and Directory*, Hillsdale, 1999, p. 2.

68. John Camper, *Detroit News*, November 12, 1967.

69. Author's interview with Mickey Craig, March 31, 2000.

70. Plato, translated by B. Jowett. *The Republic and Other Works*, New York, 1973, p. 44.

71. Author's interview with Mickey Craig, March 31, 2000.

72. Anderson, "George and Me."

73. Author's interview with Kay Cosgrove, April 1, 2000.

74. Helen Dunn Gates, *Life and Labors of Ransom Dunn,* Boston, 1901, p. 121.

75. Author's interview with Michael Poliakoff, May 19, 2000.

76. Author's interview with June Roche, March 13, 2000.

77. Author's interview with Arlan and Caroline Gilbert, March 12 and 13, 2000.

78. Author's interview with John Reist, March 26, 2000.

79. Author's interview with June Roche, March 13, 2000.

80. Author's interview with an anonymous friend of George Roche III, Spring 2000.

81. Terry Mattingly, Scripps Howard News Service in the *Jackson Citizen Patriot,* February 18, 2000.

82. George Roche, "Capitalism and the Future of America," *Imprimis,* 1988.

83. Author's interview with Mickey Craig, March 31, 2000.

84. Ibid.

85. Ibid.

86. Author's interview with June Roche, March 13, 2000.

87. Ibid.

88. Ibid.

89. Ibid.

90. Author's interview with Arlan Gilbert, August 20, 2000.

91. Ibid.

92. Ibid.

93. Author's interview with Arlan Gilbert, March 12, 2000.

94. Author's interview with confidential source, May 2000.

95. Author's interview with June Roche, March 13, 2000.

Chapter 4

96. Lissa Roche's letter of resignation, September 8, 1999.

97. Ibid.

98. Author's interview with Arlan Gilbert.

99. Author's interview with John Cervini, May 16, 2000.

100. Author's interview with Arlan Gilbert, March 12, 2000.

101. Sam Tannenhaus, "Deadly Devotion," *Vanity Fair,* March 2000.

102. Author's interviews with Dean Hagan, May 30 and June 5, 2000.

103. Ibid.

104. Ibid.

105. Author's interviews with Dean Hagan, May 30 and June 5, 2000.

106. Ibid.

107. Una Hogue, "The Life of Shavano" in *Under the Angel of Shavano,* Denver, 1963, p. 39.

108. Stella Hosmer Bailey, *The Charisma of Chalk Creek,* privately published, 1985, p. 60.

109. Hogue, in *Under the Angel of Shavano,* p. 41.

110. Corinne Harpending, *The Legend of the Angel of Shavano* (Salida), Heart of the Rockies Chamber of Commerce, no date.

111. Author's interview with John Cervini, May 16, 2000.

112. Author's interviews with Dean Hagan, May 30 and June 5, 2000.

113. Ibid.

114. Author's interview with Pia and Dan York, March 31, 2000.

115. Author's interviews with Dean Hagan, May 30 and June 5, 2000.

116. Ibid.

117. George Roche III, statement to Hillsdale Police, November 15, 1999.

118. Author's interviews with Dean Hagan, May 30 and June 5, 2000.

119. Ibid.

120. Ibid.

121. Ibid.

122. George Roche IV, Hillsdale Police Department Voluntary Statement Form, October 17, 1999.

123. John J. Miller, "Horror at Hillsdale," *National Review*

Online, November 12, 1999.

124. Hillsdale City Police Department Report, November 9, 1999. p. 17.

125. Author's interviews with Dean Hagan, May 30 and June 5, 2000.

126. Hillsdale Police Department 911 tape of George Roche IV's call.

CHAPTER 5

127. Hillsdale Police Department report, November 24, 1999, p. 4.

128. Author's interview with June Roche, March 13, 2000.

129. Hillsdale Police Department report, November 24, 1999, p. 9.

130. Ibid.

131. Hillsdale Police Department detective Bradley J. Martin's interview with George Roche IV on November 11, 1999: "George was ... asked why it was that he did not divulge the alleged affair between Lissa and his father on the day of her death. He replied that after speaking with Robert Blackstock, he thought that the affair was something he did not wish to reveal at that time."

132. Dee Drummond, "Lissa Roche Tried To Leave Hillsdale Job 6 Weeks Earlier," *Toledo Blade,* November 30, 1999.

133. Hillsdale Police Department Report, November 24, 1999, p. 18.

134. Hillsdale Police Department Report, November 24, 1999, p. 10.

135. Drummond, "Lissa Roche Tried To Leave Hillsdale Job 6 Weeks Earlier."

136. Bradley J. Martin in Hillsdale Police Department Report, November 24, 1999, p. 12.

137. Ibid.

138. Author's interview with Sgt. John Kase, Michigan State Police, July 21, 2000.

139. Hillsdale Police Department Report on the death of Lissa Roche, November 24, 1999. Cover letter.

140. Author's interview with Detective Bradley J. Martin, July 21, 2000.

141. Author's interviews with Dean Hagan, May 30 and June 5, 2000.

142. Author's interview with Detective Bradley J. Martin, July 21, 2000.

143. John J. Miller, "Horror at Hillsdale."

144. Dee Drummond in the *Toledo Blade,* "Police Say Suicide Closes Probe at Hillsdale," November 29, 2000.

145. Peggy Walsh-Sarnecki, "Hillsdale Cops Seek to Shield Former School President's Family," *Detroit Free Press,* November 30, 1999.

146. Author's interview with Detective Bradley Martin, June 12, 2000.

147. *Christian's Treasury,* edited by Lissa Roche, Wheaton, Ill., 1995, p. 84.

148. Peggy Walsh-Sarnecki, "Hillsdale Cops Seek to Shield Former School President's Family."

CHAPTER 6

149. Author's interviews with Dean Hagan, May 30 and June 6, 2000.

150. Author's interview with Michael Bauman, March 31, 2000.

151. Jennifer Frey, *Washington Post,* November 18, 1999, p. C1.

152. Hillsdale College Memo re: recent events from Dr. Robert Blackstock, November 22, 1999.

153. Author's interview with June Roche, March 13, 2000.

154. Author's interview with Michael Medved, May 16, 2000.

CHAPTER 7

155. Author's interview with Michael Bauman, March 31, 2000.

156. Author's interview with John Reist, March 26, 2000.

157. Ibid.

158. Ibid.

159. Author's interview with Michael Poliakoff, May 19, 2000.

160. Author's interview with June Roche, March 13, 2000.

161. Author's interview with John Cervini, May 16, 2000.

AFTERWORD

162. Paul Harvey, Commencement Address May 13, 2000.

HILLSDALE POLICE DEPARTMENT REPORT

163. George's younger brother is actually Jake.

LISSA ROCHE'S LETTER OF RESIGNATION

164. Gleaves Whitney was one of two finalists considered by the Hillsdale trustees in their search for a president to replace George Roche. He currently works for Michigan Governor John Engler.

Acknowledgments

Many people shared my enthusiasm for this project. Bob Drews, a wonderful editor, and designer Paula Morrison were a pleasure to work with, as was indexer Sayre Van Young. I am also grateful to my uncle Calvin Goodman who encouraged me to take on this project and made many important observations and suggestions. Anne Hagen did a superb research job on this project. Richard Harris also generously contributed his talents, as did my brother Ron, sister Carla, daughter Elizabeth, Peter Jan Honigsberg, and Linda Moyer.

The staffs of the Berkeley Public Library, the Buena Vista Library in Colorado, the Hackley Public Library in Muskegon, the Mossey Library at Hillsdale College, the Mitchell Public Library in Hillsdale, the Simon Wiesenthal Library in Los Angeles, Volume One Bookstore in Hillsdale and Little Professor Bookstore in Jackson were all particularly helpful. In addition thanks go to Vick Basra, Michael Bauman, Kendall Brown, Linda Bryant, John Cervini, Mickey Craig, Amy England, Anne English, Arlan and Caroline Gilbert, Dean Hagan, Jerry Hatton, John Juroe, Bob Koen, Shelia Kowalsky, Margot Lind, Michael Medved, Michael Poliakoff, Ed Quillen, my father Dan Rapoport, my children Jonathan and Elizabeth Rapoport, John Reist, Ted Robertson, June Roche, Dorothy Roman, Stan Sesser, Karen Shirard, Sam Spiegel, Gordana Sormaz, Peter and Pat Sussman, Lori and Mike Venturini, Charles Von Eaton, Melinda Von Sydow, John Willson, Richard Wunsch, and Pia and Dan York. To those, and others who have generously contributed to my research but prefer not to take credit for their help, I offer my sincere thanks.

Special thanks go to my colleagues at RDR Books Linda Cohen, Rick Mok and Francesca Weiss. I am indebted to many people in the Hillsdale community. All of the information contained in this book is based on direct interviews with principals who were actually present at the time of the conversations and scenes recounted in this book.

Finally, I want to mention two people whose extraordinary lives are the heart of this story. After raising more than $300 million for Hillsdale College, George Roche was not even allowed to publish a farewell letter in a campus publication. Yet without George Roche it is doubtful Hillsdale would have ever been able to have put together the extraordinary academic team that has benefited thousands of men and women. This is his most important legacy. I also want to commend the fine work of Lissa Roche. Politics aside, she was a gifted editor who was so determined to turn dross into gold that she would even, from time to time, try to rewrite the work of deceased authors. Only after her death did many people come to appreciate her important contributions to the Hillsdale community. I hope that her many accomplishments will be a source of great comfort to her family and friends and an inspiration to others.

Index

About the Author

Roger Rapoport grew up in Detroit, Michigan, and has followed educational issues around the country since his college days at the University of Michigan where he served as editor of the *Michigan Daily*. His reporting on the business relationship between the campus library and University Microfilms, a company owned by a University of Michigan regent, led to an attorney general's investigation that declared the regent in substantial conflict of interest. The regent responded by resigning his position.

The co-author of *Is The Library Burning,* a book on the student power movement in the 1960s, he has written extensively on education for many national magazines and newspapers. His writing has appeared in *Parade, The Atlantic Monthly, The New Republic, Esquire* and *Harper's.* He has also written for the *San Jose Mercury News,* the *Los Angeles Times,* the *San Francisco Chronicle,* the *Oakland Tribune* and many other newspapers. His books include a study of the nuclear weapons industry, a dual biography of California Governors Pat and Jerry Brown and a close look at Eastern Europe after the fall of the Berlin Wall. He is also co-editor of *I Should Have Stayed Home.* He lives in Berkeley, California, and thanks to the modern miracle of the commuter marriage, spends considerable time in Michigan with his wife, Martha Ferriby. He has two children, a son, Jonathan, and a daughter, Elizabeth, and a stepson, William Ferriby.